The Story of
THE LONDON BUS

Garden seat horse bus, with passengers in late Victorian costume

JOHN R. DAY

The Story of
THE
LONDON
BUS

*London and its buses from the
horse bus to the present day*

LONDON TRANSPORT

55 BROADWAY WESTMINSTER

LONDON SW1

0 85329 037 7

Set in 10 point Monotype Baskerville (Series 169)
Printed and bound in England by
STAPLES PRINTERS LIMITED
at The Stanhope Press, Rochester, Kent.

Contents

'Winged-wheel' symbol of the L.G.O.C.

AUTHOR'S NOTE

*This book was originally intended to be no more than an
up-dating of 'London General', published by London Transport
in 1956 to mark the centenary of the London General Omnibus
Company, but it soon became evident that something much more
comprehensive was needed to tell, even in broad outline,
the full story of the London bus. The earlier book,
nevertheless, was the foundation on which the present volume
was built and I acknowledge the debt I owe to its authors.*

*I should also like to thank all my colleagues in London
Transport who have been good enough to read the proofs and
make suggestions for improvements.   Special thanks are due to
Mr. Charles E. Lee, whose detailed knowledge of London bus
history and painstaking scrutiny of detail has been
invaluable.   Thanks are also due to Miss J. Reed for
undertaking, over a considerable period, the typing of
the original manuscript.*

John R. Day

Enfield 1973

Introduction

The buses of London are so familiar a sight that it seems as though there could never have been a time when they were not part of the everyday scene. Old films, old photographs of London streets show buses – horse or motor – everywhere. But there was a time when London had no buses at all. The only public transport was by stage coach, by hackney carriage, or by river boat. Some of the coaches ran on 'short' stages from what are now the inner suburbs or even part of London itself but at that time were well out of London, but booking in advance was usually needed. The hackney carriages (dating from the 1630s) had a monopoly on the paved roads of London and the short-stage coaches were not allowed to pick up or set down passengers in the area of the 'stones', as they were called, except at the terminus of a route.

The hackney carriages, now the taxicabs of London, no longer have a monopoly. This book tells the story of the beginning and development of the Londoner's most-used means of travel – the London bus.

I How the Bus Began

THE story of the London bus – indeed of all buses the world over – began in France more than three hundred years ago when Blaise Pascal, under letters patent granted by Louis XIV, ran the first of his 'carrosses à cinq sols' on 18 March 1662 over a fixed route at a fixed fare in Paris. These 'five-sou carriages' were not yet called 'omnibuses' – that name was to come much later, though also from France – but they held themselves open for the carriage of all comers (or nearly all, since peasants and soldiers were specifically excluded by the letters patent). The vehicles held eight passengers and those on the first route were shortly joined by others on four more routes selected, just as one might choose today, to serve the business and administrative areas of the Paris of the time. One circular route, longer than the others, had five-sou fare stages. Timetables were published for all routes, showing that the two-horse vehicles, decked in the royal arms, ran every seven or eight minutes. The timetables were also devised to give interchange between routes at suitable points.

It will be seen that practically every feature of a bus service today was introduced in one grand gesture in 1662 by Pascal, man of mathematics and religion, in this the last year of his life. As it happens, the letters patent were held not by Pascal himself but by his friend and patron the Duc de Roannez. For this reason the services were able to continue for twenty years after their inventor's death until the ageing Duc de Roannez surrendered his monopoly. Had Pascal lived, the bus services he originated might have been expanded, but in effect they died after this short but notable life and had to be invented all over again.

According to *The Public Advertiser* of 18 January 1772, vehicles resembling buses were considered for introduction into London in that year. They would have carried 14 passengers between Charing Cross and the Royal Exchange at a fare of 6d. There were at that time already more than 1,000 hackney carriages for hire, to say nothing of sedan chairs which had been introduced, at about the same time as the hackney carriages, in the early 17th century and were still to be seen as late as the beginning of the 19th century. The 1772 buses seem not to have appeared – at least in recognizable form – but something of

[1]

Shillibeer's horse bus outside his coachbuilder's shop in Bury Street, Bloomsbury.
Passengers boarded at a centre door in the rear of the bus

the sort did grow up in the shape of the short-stage coaches. The long-distance stage coach is something of romance and memory, but the short-stage coaches were the ones which took people from a local booking office (and sometimes even from their homes) to a stopping place on the long-stage routes. They also distributed passengers from the long-stage point in similar fashion.

Soon the connection with the long-stage coach disappeared and the short-stage services carried on in their own right. In London they normally ran from points in the City or West End out to the suburbs, carrying pre-booked passengers at a fixed fare. But there were more and more would-be passengers who were picked up at the roadside and carried – after hot arguments about the fare – for only part of the journey. In 1825 over 400 short-stage coaches left from the City every day to such destinations as Edmonton, Hammersmith, Hackney, Islington, and Padding-ton. Paddington was by far the most popular destination, catering for the monied travellers from their homes beside the New Road. Costs and fares were high, for the coach proprietors had to pay a considerable amount in duties. They were handicapped, too, in not being allowed to set down or pick up passengers once they reached the paved streets of London – or the 'stones', as they were known.

Once the 'stones' were reached the hackney carriages had a monopoly – established in the first place to prevent street congestion in the City. There was thus a gap between what the stage vehicles could provide and the hackney coach services. Most of the hackney coaches at this time were in a poor state but lighter vehicles coming nearer in spirit – and speed – to the modern taxicab were being introduced. The end of the Napoleonic wars saw considerable street improvements in London and three new bridges were opened over the

*A facsimile of the Shillibeer vehicle on display at Clapham
and now in the London Transport Collection at Syon Park*

Thames. The turnpikes also vanished from the inner London streets, making it possible at long last to make, for example, a journey from one end of Oxford Street to the other without having to pay a toll. These improvements began to make nonsense of the fear of congestion that lay behind the hackney carriage monopoly and it was ended in 1832, opening the door to the omnibus.

Yet to arrive at the London omnibus we must go back to Paris, where in 1819 Jacques Lafitte, banker and politician, introduced omnibuses on short routes across the city. These carried 16–18 passengers, all inside, at a fare roughly equivalent to 1p. They proved very successful – so much so that the first year's profits are said to have repaid the original outlay. They were still not called omnibuses, however. For that we must look south-westwards to Nantes, where Stanislas Baudry was running a vehicle like those of Lafitte between Nantes and the suburb of

Richebourg, where he owned hot baths. His terminus in Nantes was either at or near the shop of a grocer named Omnes, who painted on the fascia board over the shop the name 'Omnes omnibus'. Baudry adopted the name 'Omnibus' and used it when in January 1828 the Paris police authorized him, with two friends, to operate 100 coaches on ten routes through Paris.

The Baudry concern was called 'L'Entreprise des Omnibus' and used 14-passenger vehicles divided into three classes with a separate fare for each class. It had an immediate success with the public even though only half the permitted 100 omnibuses were put into service. Other proprietors soon sprang up to take up the remaining licences and the name 'omnibus' was soon thoroughly established. Unfortunately it seems that the Paris winter of 1829 was a particularly hard one and the price of forage for the horses was very high. The streets were almost impassable and the buses could not run. Baudry, bankrupt and ruined, committed suicide – a sad fate for a worthy pioneer.

The longer-established and better-financed omnibuses of the Lafitte establishment, however, weathered this particular storm. In the autumn of the previous year (1828) Lafitte had ventured to introduce two very superior vehicles under the name 'Les Dames Blanches'. The name was taken from Boieldieu's opera 'La Dame Blanche', which had appeared in 1825 and was especially popular at that time. The omnibuses were painted white and the harness and driver's livery were mainly white. There was even a sort of mechanical horn which played themes from the opera. The two coaches are important because there may have been some connection between them and the first true London omnibuses. Some versions have it that George Shillibeer, of whom much more later, was in business as a coach-builder in Paris and was employed by Lafitte to build 'Les Dames Blanches'. He himself claimed in 1830 that he had premises in Paris and had built omnibuses for Lafitte. Other accounts say that he saw and was impressed by the new vehicles. If he built 'Les Dames Blanches' he would have been 30–31 at the time, and at the age of 33 he certainly had, in partnership with John Cavill, a coachbuilding business in Bloomsbury. He was also a livery stable keeper and he had definite connections with Paris, so he was no small figure. He had also been trying to secure licences to run public vehicles for some years, culminating in the 'memorial' he sent to the Treasury in July 1828. Though doomed to failure by the hackney carriage monopoly, the 'memorial' is worth quoting as the shape of things to come. It leaves no doubt of Shillibeer's debt to Paris:

'Your Memorialist has no doubt but that your Lordships have heard of the new public vehicle, called *Omnibus* recently established at *Paris* and authorised by an ordonnance from the Prefecture of Police to convey passengers without luggage to and from the barriers of Paris at the moderate charge of 5 sous or 2½d for a course of about one mile and a half English.

'Your Memorialist having been to Paris for the purpose of viewing these carriages which commenced running about two months since, and being impressed by ocular demonstration of their extreme utility in London, contemplating establishing them in London under the more English name of Economist, their convenience being so greatly acknowledged at Paris notwithstanding there are 1,700 hackney coaches and 900 cabriolets in that city. It is with the strongest impression of their utility here, where the expense of conveyance is so high that the industrious part of the community are obliged to walk, that your Memorialist most humbly begs to solicit your Lordships' sanction to work these carriages upon the most frequented routes of the Metropolis according to the plan which your Memorialist has now the honour to submit, each vehicle being built to contain 18 persons, *all inside* without any luggage, to be drawn by three horses abreast, having a decent coachman on the box and a well-conducted man inside as receiver, the price of each course being at the rate of less than 3d. per mile and subject to any regulations your Lordships may deem necessary to adopt, the object of your Memorialist being to give the public a safe and comfortable conveyance over the London stones at one fourth the price of the present hackney carriages.'

Not to be outdone by the failure of his Memorial, and possibly realizing that the end of the hackney carriage monopoly was in sight and that the sooner his ideas could be seen working in practice the better, Shillibeer turned his attention to the New Road – consisting of the present Marylebone, Euston, and Pentonville Roads and lying mostly beyond the 'stones'. This route had heavy traffic, including much from the Paddington/Marylebone area where, although not many people could afford to keep their own carriages, there were many who could well afford to travel in a Shillibeer omnibus. Along this route, too, except right at the City end where the New Road ended at the Angel, Islington, passengers could be picked up or set down at will. In April 1829, Shillibeer let it be known that he was building two omnibuses – the word 'Economist' seems soon to have been forgotten – for service between Paddington and the Bank via the New Road.

On 4 July 1829 his first omnibus began to run, and on the same day *The British Traveller* carried an advertisement which repeated Shillibeer's debt to Paris and emphasized the respectability of his omnibus and its suitability for the carriage of ladies and children – not generally features of the short-stage coaches of the time. The advertisement read:

'OMNIBUS

G. SHILLIBEER, induced by the universal admiration the above vehicle called forth at Paris, has commenced running one upon the Parisian mode from PADDINGTON to the BANK.

'The superiority of the Carriage over the ordinary Stage Coaches, for comfort and safety, must be obvious, all the Passengers being Inside and the Fare charged from Paddington to the Bank being One Shilling, and from Islington to the Bank or Paddington Sixpence.

'The Proprietor begs to add, that a person of great respectability attends his Vehicle as Conductor; and every possible attention will be paid to the accommodation of Ladies and Children.

'Hours of starting:– From Paddington Green to the Bank at 9, 12, 3, 6, and 8 o'clock; from the Bank to Paddington at 10, 1, 4, 7, and 9 o'clock.'

The Shillibeer omnibuses – there were two from August 1 – were certainly much better than the general run of short-stage coaches running at the time. They were drawn by three horses and the conductors were smart young men, personable and dressed in something not unlike a naval midshipman's uniform. It was put about that they were the sons of naval officer friends of Shillibeer's.

The Press received them well, the *Morning Post* of 7 July 1829 reporting: 'Saturday the new vehicle, called the *Omnibus*, commenced running from Paddington to the City, and excited considerable notice, both from the novel form of the carriage and the elegance with which it is fitted out. It is capable of accommodating 16 or 18 persons, all inside; and we apprehend it would be almost impossible to make it overturn, owing to the great

George Shillibeer

width of the carriage. It was drawn by three beautiful bays abreast, after the French fashion. The *Omnibus* is a handsome machine, in the shape of a van, with windows on each side, and one at the end. The width the horses occupy will render the vehicle rather inconvenient to be turned, or driven through some of the streets of London.'

The number of seats in the Shillibeer omnibus has long been a matter of conjecture. The (presumably) eye-witness account above gives 16 or 18 – possibly depending on the width of the passengers – but the figure of 22

The horse bus serving the new Birmingham Railway, Euston, about 1850

has often been stated. A careful contemporary account in the *Mechanics' Magazine* of 8 August 1829 makes it more probable that the actual number was 20.

Shillibeer's success, apart from the better vehicles and superior crews, was probably due mainly to the lower and regular fare (which, unlike some other coaches, was applied without argument, bickering, or bartering) and his insistence on punctuality. His omnibuses did not wait around at the regular stops for more passengers but went on, full or not. Also, his omnibuses provided full protection from the weather. The rivals on the route, on which there were already more than 160 journeys a day, charged 1s. 6d.–2s. for inside passengers, with a reduction of sixpence for those travelling on the roof. The average capacity seems to have been 4–6 inside and

seven on the roof, so that by any count Shillibeer's omnibuses were bigger and more comfortable. They also had three horses against the two of the coaches, and no pre-booking was required.

It has to be confessed that the two 'midshipmen' were largely window-dressing, for once their initial effect had been made they were replaced by two other conductors in a velvet livery. These must have been better than the usual run, however, and in August the *Morning Advertiser* was able to write that the short-stage coachmen of Paddington, 'who heretofore were proverbial for their rudeness and ruffianism, are now being rapidly metamorphosed into civil and attentive personages. This miracle is being wrought by the introduction of . . . the Omnibus'.

[6]

This could well have been the start of the tradition of superior conductors of Paddington, one of whom, rather later in time, was celebrated in song as having married Pretty Polly Perkins of Paddington Green.

Shillibeer's success did not go unmarked. Others were quick to copy. The Hammersmith–Hyde Park Corner–St. Paul's route run by George Cloud, for example, had omnibuses by May 1830. These were two-horse coaches giving easier manoevrability in the City streets and were rather smaller than Shillibeer's – who himself had been obliged, either because of the width of the three-horse arrangement or for reasons of economy, to bring his motive power down to two horses. Shillibeer probably did not have the capital to exploit his success, for although by mid-1830 he had six omnibuses on the Paddington–Bank route others were catching up and in 1831 there were 90 omnibuses on this single route of which only 12 were Shillibeer's.

The competition made difficulties for Shillibeer on the route he had pioneered along the New Road. In March 1831 he was declared bankrupt, though he seems to have continued to look after the business – possibly as, in effect, a manager. He was elected chairman, in September 1831, of a group or association of proprietors who got together to regulate the cut-throat competition on the New Road route which had led to racing between omnibuses and fighting for passengers by conductors. The association recommended the appointment of 'regulators' who were to see that buses were properly spaced out along the route, the cutting of the number of buses from 90 to 57, and the establishment of a regular three-minute interval service from 0800 to 2200.

From 5 January 1832, a change came over the scene. From that date short stage carriages were allowed to stop to set down or take up passengers anywhere along the route for which they had been licensed, including the central London streets which until then had been forbidden by the hackney coach monopoly. Shillibeer responded by diverting some of his Paddington–Bank buses via Oxford Street. Buses were licensed by the Commissioners of Stamps, who were more concerned with the collection of fees than the routes worked. Fees were payable on the capacity of the vehicle and also on the number of miles it covered – Shillibeer had occasion to ask for relief from, or time to pay, both these duties in 1831.

Shillibeer seems to have retired from the western routes and competition in 1834, though he ran a daily coach to Brighton. He also began a service between London, Greenwich, and Woolwich, where there was less competition – at least from other road interests. Unfortunately for him, a cheap and efficient steamer service began operating on the Thames the following year and the year after that (1836) part of the London & Greenwich Railway opened.

Unable to meet his debts, Shillibeer fled to France. On his return he was committed to the Fleet prison. He found work on his release (with the London & Southampton Railway) but was back in prison not long after on a charge relating to smuggled brandy. He found a new niche as a director of funerals in the Parisian style and designed a very successful hearse which became known as a 'Shillibeer', somewhat to the discomfort of his earlier bus rivals who had imitated him by painting the name 'shillibeer' – with a small 's' and a very small 'not' in front of it – to share in his original popularity. He seems to have continued to have various connections with buses but ended his days primarily as a funeral director. He died in 1866 and is buried in the churchyard at Chigwell. A tablet in the church, erected by the busmen of London on the occasion of the centenary of the Omnibus in 1929, hails him as the 'Inventor of the London Omnibus'. He was, it states, 'a model employer and served his day and generation well'.

[7]

*Hancock's 'Automaton' of 1836, said to have achieved
21 m.p.h. and to have been capable of carrying 30 passengers
and drawing an 18-seater trailer*

II Onward from Shillibeer

BEFORE we move on too far we must look back a year or two to 1833, when, after demonstration running of an experimental service between Stratford and London to show the fitness of his vehicle for bus work, Walter Hancock helped the London & Paddington Steam Carriage Company to run a public service of steam buses along the New Road route. This was a remarkable enterprise for so early a date – it was only three years after the opening of the Liverpool & Manchester Railway had ushered in the Age of Steam on the railways – and the railway locomotive had a considerable development period behind it which the road locomotive lacked.

This lack of development may have caused the premature demise of the steam bus, for after Hancock's first 14-seater, the 'Enterprise', which began working on 22 April 1833, had been running for a short period there was a quarrel between Hancock and the company because the company did not show enough alacrity in ordering the other two buses. Hancock took over the running himself for the summer of 1833 and that of

1834. The 'Enterprise' was the first mechanically-propelled vehicle to be designed especially for bus work. It had no seats on the roof and the driver sat on an exposed platform at the front, which also served to give entry into the main body, which resembled a railway coach in many ways, with the machinery tucked away in a massive 'boot' at the back.

The steam bus seems not to have run in 1835, but in 1836 three of them were at work – one of them a 22-seater. Apart from any mechanical difficulties they may have had, it appears that the steam buses were not popular with the public – they may have been nervous of them when they compared them with the familiar and reliable horse. Takings were low, and legislation made things even more difficult for mechanical vehicles. With a little more capital behind them, and a little more luck, the steam buses might have become more popular, more reliable, and have brought a better return for the money invested in them. It is on record that Hancock's 'Automaton', which appeared in October 1836, made a trial run from the City Road to Epping at an average speed of about

11½ m.p.h. It had wheel steering and the seats ran across the bus instead of along it as in the horse vehicles. The *Morning Herald* of 25 October 1836 recorded that 'Automaton' entered Epping 'amidst the loud cheers of some thousands who were collected in the town, it being market day . . .', astonishing those 'who could not imagine how it was moved without horses'. A sad end to enterprise – all the steam buses were taken off the road before the end of 1840.

The general horse-bus scene in the later

according to Charles Dickens, was sometimes wont to entice or even 'help' a passenger inside without making it very clear where his particular bus was going. Such a case was tried at Mansion House on 30 June 1849, when the Clerk stated that more than 4,000 summonses had been issued against bus conductors in the preceding year.

Fares at the time seem to have remained at sixpence, with three pence for the half journey (hence the name 'Threepenny Omnibuses') and a shilling for exceptionally long

Three of Walter Hancock's steam carriages of the 1830s

Shillibeer years and for some time after was confused – and probably confusing for the public of the time. The early, very superior, buses seem to have petered out and most of the vehicles were 'boxes on wheels' drawn by two horses and seating 12 inside and three on top next to the driver. The conductor, or 'cad' as he was often known (for no very obvious reason unless it was because their dress, and that of the drivers, was so shabby) stood on a step at the back and took the fares. He, with the driver's connivance, often held the bus for more passengers if he thought fit, and,

journeys to the fringes. There were very many bus owners, each having one or two vehicles one of which they often drove themselves. The Stage Carriage Act of 1832 made it compulsory for vehicles to be licensed and largely because of the practice of hanging about for extra passengers with subsequent delays to those already on the bus, it became compulsory from 10 August 1838 for drivers and conductors to be licensed also, and to wear their licence numbers in a prominent position – as they still have to do today. This enabled offenders to be readily identified and they could be fined for causing an obstruction. The buses had to carry the Stamp Office number, the number of passengers for which they were licensed, and the words 'Metropolitan Stage Carriage'.

In effect, however, the regulations were not severe enough to deter anyone with a small amount of capital from buying a bus or two, a small stud of horses, and hiring suitable men and premises. For the drivers and conductors there was no test of skill or aptitude – only a character reference and the declaration of age, name, and address. The writing was on the wall, however, to a sufficient extent to get some proprietors to join together in associations similar to the successful pioneer one on the New Road route and in 1838 an association not tied to any particular route was formed as a means of self-protection against further Parliamentary interference. The proprietors themselves continued to flout regulations, packing in as many passengers as they could, regardless of the official limits.

The main function of the associations was to curb competition and bring some sort of order into the free-for-all on the route in question, or sometimes a related group of routes. When an association had been formed, the name was painted on all its buses and the buses themselves were generally all painted in one colour. The service was organized to run at agreed intervals and each owner was allotted a number of 'times' at which he could run, the number varying according to the number of buses controlled by each owner. In this way everyone knew when his buses should be running and no-one would poach on his 'times'. These 'times' became a saleable commodity, like goodwill, and were part of the purchase price for the new entrant if an existing proprietor wished to sell out.

All the receipts were pooled and shared out according to the number of buses involved. This made sure that a proprietor given two profitable rush-hour 'times' and two unprofitable 'times' at slack periods did not conveniently fail to work the unprofitable

journeys. If the association thought that there were too many buses for the traffic offering, it could stand off some vehicles, the owners being paid a fixed compensation each week.

Some of the associations grew very large and powerful, particularly, in later years, the Atlas & Waterloo, with which two famous bus names, Birch and Tilling, were associated, as well as the London General Omnibus Company itself.

The routes with the largest number of buses at this period were still the original pioneer route between Paddington and the City via the New Road and its later, and even busier, variant via Oxford Street. Some companies were formed with quite large fleets – for example, the dominant operator on the Oxford Street route was the London Conveyance Company, which lasted from 1836 to 1852. It was closely associated with the biggest company of all, Blore & Co. Another large company was the Richmond Conveyance Company, which was formed in 1844 and lasted until 1865, when its business was acquired by the London General Omnibus Company for £4,900. One of the largest fleets to grow up was that of E. & J. Wilson who ran the famous 'Favorite' line of omnibuses, their main routes being from North London to the City and Central London. In the early 1850s Wilson's marked May 1 each year by a procession of buses – a popular event.

An illustration of one of this firm's buses in the 1840s shows that a second row of four seats had been added on top behind the driver and in 1847 Adams & Company began to build a bus with a clerestory roof which offered a convenient 'back-to-back' seat running the length of the roof as well as giving more headroom and better ventilation inside. It had already been the custom for a year or two to scramble, in the rush hour, on to such buses as had curved roofs and sit back-to-back along the centre, so the clerestory was provided with iron safety arms at each end, a low board was put along each edge of the roof as a footrest. The roof became a regular resort

A 'knifeboard' bus about 1860

of male passengers, encouraged at first by being charged only half the inside fare. These buses with proper roof seats (though access was by the athletic climbing of a series of iron rungs) were a good deal heavier than the standard form of bus and consequently slow to gain acceptance. The process was speeded up, however, by the traffic which poured into London for the Great Exhibition of 1851. Bus owners began to fit long boards along the centre of the roof to act as back-to-back seating, and as there were younger ladies daring enough to travel on the roof 'decency boards' were added along the roof edges. They served not only to hide dainty ankles from the gaze of pedestrians but also to carry advertisements. These long seats, from their appearance, were generally known as 'knifeboards' – which everyone used in those days to sharpen up the carving knife for the Sunday joint – and they remained, in gradually improving form, for over thirty years. Steps to the upper deck, if we may now call it that, did not come into general use until 1882.

On 1 November 1850, the *Evening Standard* reported: 'In consequence of the overcrowd-ing on the roofs of certain omnibuses, and the danger and indecency of such a mode of passenger traffic, the Commissioners of Police have intimated to the proprietors of omnibuses generally their intention of doing away with the seats on the roofs of these vehicles.' But the omnibus proprietors made a successful appeal against the police order, and the roof continued to be used.

The 'knifeboard' was not the only innovation. J. A. Franklinski, of Franklinski's Patent Omnibus & Cabriolet Company, for example, produced a bus in which every passenger travelled in his or her own little cubicle, with a voice-tube to get in touch with the conductor. There were steps to what was described as a 'gallery' on top which again had a separate door to each compartment. This bus actually ran for a period in 1851 between Charing Cross and Bayswater, but it must have been very heavy.

An idea of the commotion caused by the 1851 exhibition, with some sidelights on Franklinski's bus, can be gained from this short extract from Yvonne ffrench's *The Great Exhibition: 1851*. She writes, 'May-

[11]

day had been declared a public holiday. . . . Throughout most of London, shopkeepers had put up their shutters, and having no customers had gone off to see the show. Omnibuses were plying in one direction, all placarded "To the Exhibition" with new reins and rosettes on their horses, and button-holes and streamers in the coats and on the whips of the drivers.

'From every quarter of London they were arriving, each with their distinctive names, "Paragon" and "Waterloo", "Atlas" and "Camberwell". There were the almost defunct Shillibeers and the new improved Franklinskis. For mass transport was still in its infancy and the one thing the public seems to have wanted was to get away from its neighbour. Franklinski's omnibus was a determined attempt to solve the problem . . . .'

Mention of the speaking tube recalls that the bell which could be rung from a cord inside the bus was produced as early as 1839 by a London firm, Holzapfel & Co., but failed to win popularity. The more usual method, if method there was at all, was to provide two straps, one attached to the driver's right arm and the other to his left. One pulled one strap or the other according to whether one wished to be set down on the left of the road or the right – there was no such thing as the 'rule-of-the-road' in those days. More often, there was no device and one shouted to the conductor or snatched at his sleeve or, regrettably, poked him with a walking stick.

Another odd bus was the 'Curvilinear' by W. C. Scott, which had 13 seats with backs curved to form-fitting shape as in some motorcars today – but in wood, not soft upholstery. It also had foot-guards to prevent passengers treading on each others toes and had clips for newspapers. (Newspapers had been provided on other buses, but were discontinued when so many were stolen. The *Sunday Times* for 30 November 1851 describes their introduction on the 'Islington omnibuses' and explains that passengers were expected to put a penny in a box for the pleasure of reading them.) Scott's bus, as had

Franklinski's before it, had a device for counting passengers. This seems to have been designed to protect the owner's revenue by ensuring that receipts tallied with passengers carried rather than to ensure comfortable conditions without overcrowding inside the bus, and it did not work for long.

The public showed no great enthusiasm for these innovations and they quietly vanished away.

The Commissioners of Excise took over the collection of duties on stage carriages on 4 October 1847 from the Commissioners of Stamps, and an even more important event occurred soon afterwards when the Metropolitan Police took over the duties of the Metropolitan Public Carriages Office in April 1850. This paved the way for the Commissioners of Excise to make the granting of a licence subject to a satisfactory report on the vehicle by the police.

There can be little doubt that the year 1851 marked a turning point in the career of the London bus. It introduced many who had not used such a vehicle before to its possibilities and – sometimes – pleasures. An illustrated Omnibus Guide, with drawings of the bus sides, with lettering, for route identification was published in May 1851. It gave a fascinating insight into the services already available. Among the services listed, with names in huge letters along the side of the vehicles, were geographical descriptions such as: Bayswater; Blackwall; Brentford; Brompton; Chelsea; Clapton Gate; Upper Clapton; Knightsbridge Islington & Holloway; Edmonton; Exhibition; Exhibition Hyde Park; Paddington; Old Kent Road; Hackney; Oxford Street; Hounslow; Islington; Islington & Kent Road; Kensal Green; Kensington; Kew Bridge; King's Cross; Norwood; Pimlico; Waterloo; Westminster; Putney; Richmond; and Turnham Green.

Then there were the associations and companies: Brentford & Hammersmith Association; Camberwell & Dulwich Conveyance Association; Bank, Holborn, Oxford Street, Pantheon Conveyance Association; New

*The Paddington Conveyance Association bus which also served
the South Eastern Railway at London Bridge, about 1845*

Road Conveyance Association; Paddington Conveyance Association; Hampstead Conveyance Company; Richmond Conveyance Company; the Conveyance Society (Highgate Hill – Whitechapel); Holborn, Bank, Oxford Street Conveyance Society; and last of all, in anticipation, the L.C.C. – which in this case stood for the London Conveyance Company. The railways themselves ran buses – sometimes only for railway passengers with through tickets but often for all. The Great Northern Railway, for example, had a route between King's Cross and Charing Cross via 'Gray's-inn-lane, Holborn-bars, along Holborn to Long-acre, St. Martin's-lane, Charing-cross'. The fare was 6d., which included 40 lb. of luggage, but a warning note said 'Heavy luggage is a matter of agreement as to the charge between the passenger and the conductor; but the company's servant will interfere if thought to be excessive'. The buses, bearing the words 'By Appointment' over the windows, awaited the arrival of trains at King's Cross. They left Charing Cross half an hour before the advertised departure time of the train from King's Cross. Luggage was carried on the roof. 'These Omnibuses', said the *Illustrated Omnibus Guide*, 'are under the control of the company, and are well conducted.' The Great Northern also ran buses between King's Cross and London Bridge, and between King's Cross and Elephant & Castle.

The Great Western Railway also ran 'By Appointment' buses between Paddington and various inns and booking offices in the City and West End. 'On the arrival of the evening parliamentary train', stated one notice, 'there is one to the Elephant & Castle, Kennington'.

Foremost in popular appeal, however, came the imaginative names of bus history: Paragon, Nelson, Royal Blue, Plenipo, Albion, Wellington, Favorite, Times, Enchantress, British Queen, Atlas, City Atlas, and Magnet. And of course, the proper names, some full of music, some dull, like 'Taglioni' and 'Crump' and 'Hardwick'.

Or one could commute in style from the suburbs. Even in this year of 1851 one could travel the 17½ miles from the Thatched House, Epping to The Bull, Aldgate in time for the busy day at the office and leave for home again at four in the afternoon. But the boom traffic of the exhibition left its legacy in memories of decrepit vehicles and animals dragged out for quick profit-making, in recollections of exorbitant fares – especially for those who wanted to get back from the exhibition – and of the congestion in the streets both from genuine omnibuses and the miscellany of other vehicles brought out to serve as omnibuses for the occasion. There were calls in the Press for reform and re-organization, the technical journal *The Builder* in particular, as early as October 1851, calling prophetically for a reorganiz-ation on the lines adopted in Paris. Bus traffic slumped from the exhibition days down

to, and even below, the former level. Competition between bus-owners became fierce and fares were cut down not only to, but below the pre-1851 levels. The practice had been to charge a basic fare for a whole route with a half fare for half the distance, as we have seen, but in the crisis in which the industry found itself the owners agreed among themselves to divide some routes into sections and charge for those sections at separate fares. Penny fares appeared on some sections in the winter of 1851–52 and seem to have raised traffic as well as encouraging the 'hop-on-a-bus' attitude which was a feature of the London scene for so many years – and to some extent still is.

The new competition and new ways proved too much for some of the older companies, and the outbreak of the Crimean war began to raise the price of fodder for the horses. The requirement of police inspection of vehicles, which became law in 1853, also meant expenditure on keeping omnibuses in good repair – there could be no question of reducing maintenance in bad times.

The number of omnibuses in service began to fall. By 1856 it was only just over 800, despite the fact that pleas from the omnibus owners for the reduction of the mileage duty during the past few years – including a delegation sent to put their plight before Gladstone, then Chancellor of the Exchequer – had at last resulted (in 1855) in its being reduced to 1d. a mile instead of 1½d.

It was at this time that London eyes turned again to what had been happening in Paris.

III The Birth of the London General Omnibus Company

THE omnibus companies of Paris had been pursuing their own way and had found it necessary to amalgamate and band together for greater efficiency and self-protection. They were down to 11 in number when in May 1854 the Prefect of Police suggested to the *Commission Municipale* that all the companies should be merged into a single undertaking which should be granted monopoly rights. The *Commission* agreed and granted a thirty-year monopoly to the new undertaking which – after some difficulties in persuading some of the companies to join – was established under the name of the *Compagnie Générale des Omnibus* in February 1855. Services began under the new name on 1 March 1855.

A visitor to Paris during the Exhibition of 1855 – from which the Paris buses greatly benefited – was Sir Edwin Chadwick, who had made a name for himself as an administrator of note and was at that time serving on a Society of Arts sub-committee studying one of the most important town-planning concepts ever known – the plans for the rebuilding of Paris. Chadwick met and talked to a French businessman – Léopold Foucaud – with whom he discussed, among other things, the organization of the London omnibuses. Foucaud already had a great interest in the subject and was working with Joseph Orsi in an attempt to get the London companies to amalgamate. Orsi had been one of the main forces behind the Paris amalgamation and he no doubt saw monetary advantages in a similar merger in London (French money was being freely invested abroad at this time and Orsi was already in partnership in a London firm of metal dealers). The impression given to Chadwick was that all was already arranged (or almost so) and that all that remained was the shouting.

In fact, things were not quite so far advanced, but *The Times* printed a report in November 1855 to the effect that the 'London General Omnibus Company' formation was going well and that 500 buses would have been purchased by it by the beginning of 1856. A report a month earlier, but without the company name, had suggested that Foucaud and Orsi were prepared to pay £500 for each omnibus acquired complete with horses and goodwill (i.e. the 'times').

There was a great deal of opposition to the French takeover bid, not only from many of the proprietors but also from the busmen themselves, who posted placards calling on the public to keep the foreign invaders out as though the ghosts of Napoleon and the Old Guard were hovering over the New Road. Most of the opposition died away when it became known that fair prices would be paid and the existing busmen would continue to work the routes taken over. In December, the *Compagnie Générale des Omnibus de Londres* was formed in Paris by two Acts dated the 4th and 17th, Orsi and Foucaud having anticipated events a little by declaring that they already had 600 or so of London's omnibuses in their possession. The company was formed by Foucaud and Orsi with Felix Carteret. There were to be three managers, one of whom was Carteret but the other two were English omnibus proprietors – Alfred McNamara and James Willing. John Wilson, one of the largest proprietors, was named as a District Manager, as were three other proprietors. The managers (really managing directors – the French term is *gérant*) were guided (or watched over) by a *Conseil de Surveillance* divided into Paris and London sections, one of the London members being Chadwick. Sir Cusack P. Roney, better known for his railway associations, seems to have acted as a financial adviser and was for a time a London member of the *Conseil*. (The first staff were also ex-railwaymen).

With the arrival of funds from Paris the

The 'Favorite', which ran from Hornsey to Charing Cross

takeovers began – first with those proprietors who had already thrown in their lot with the new company. The way was clear for a new start and a new era in which, as *The Times* assured its readers, there would be an end to racing omnibuses, fares would be reduced, and 'an unceasing current of omnibuses would be kept in motion, succeeding one another as rapidly as the wants of the public might render necessary'. There were no more cries of 'Keep the Frenchies out'. The Frenchies were in, though it was their managers in London who dealt with most of the acquisitions. One difficulty proved to be that the purchase of the 'times' was in no sense a purchase of a monopoly, for anyone satisfying the conditions could apply for a new licence, but this seems not to have been insuperable

in practice, though it did cause the new company to revise – downwards – the payment it made for the 'times'.

The proprietors who supported the new company handed over their own vehicles – McNamara was one of the first with six omnibuses on the Kingsland–Bank and Stoke Newington–Bank routes, and he brought with him buses owned by other proprietors on the same routes as well as five from the Hackney route. In all, 27 omnibuses came under the new company on 7 January 1856, and were paid for at £510 each. On the same day, 48 omnibuses of Wilson's 'Favorite' fleet from the Highbury area were worked by the new company, though not officially handed over until January 13. Wilson received only £500 for each bus, but he received considerable

'Knifeboard' bus, now in the London Transport Collection at Syon Park

sums also for premises and equipment. And so the tale went on. The full list of all the omnibuses acquired by the new company through Foucaud and Orsi in 1856 can be found in one of the appendices to Volume I of the very comprehensive 'History of London Transport' by T. C. Barker and Michael Robbins, published by George Allen & Unwin.

By the end of the first three months nearly half London's omnibuses were in the hands of the new company. The pace then slackened, and it would seem that the competitive strength of the company may have been the persuading factor in at least some of the further sales. At the end of 1856 just over 600 omnibuses of the capital's 810 had been taken over. It was decided not to continue efforts to

buy up the rest and Orsi and Foucaud, who seem to have done very well for themselves in acting as contractors to the company in making the purchases, were given a sum – agreed by arbitration – to compensate them for the loss of profit to themselves in not purchasing the remaining omnibuses.

The managers now found themselves responsible for operating an omnibus empire of unprecedented size and having to evolve a means of controlling it and turning it to profit while providing the sort of services Londoners were expecting. The company had paid out some £400,000 – no less than £242,000 of which was for the 'times' – and results were expected, especially from the *Conseil* in Paris representing the shareholders who had provided the money. One of the first things needed was to reduce internal matters to a standard form so that the performance of various routes and the expenses of running them could be compared, like with like. All the premises had to be inspected and brought into proper repair. In some cases new stables had to be built and veterinary surgeons appointed in order to keep the horses in good condition for a longer period and so cut costs. With the same object in view, strenuous efforts were made to cut the price of fodder – equivalent to the fuel costs of today – for the 6,000 or so horses.

A central depot was set up at Spitalfields for the preparation of fodder and this was soon followed by three others, the whole fleet being supplied with a standardized mixture from these four depots, later reduced to the original Spitalfields depot and another at Paddington. The former fodder depot at Highbury became the company's main repair centre for omnibuses, and some were built there, again reducing costs.

As well as taking steps to improve the motive power by improving the quality of the stud of horses, the managers took a look at the quality of the vehicles they had taken over and seem not to have been too pleased at what they saw in relationship to demands from Paris for results. They offered, on 1 January 1856, a prize of £100 for a better omnibus design. The closing date, stated the advertisement, was to be February 2, and what was wanted was the best design and specification 'for an omnibus that, with the same weight as at present, will afford increased space accommodation and comfort to the public'. The advertisement was placed by 'Macnamara, F. Carteret, Willing, & Co.' a curious description which suggests that another title for the company may have been held in reserve. The 'General' is said to have been a last-minute addition to the name 'London General Omnibus Company' inspired by the rival registration in November 1855 of the 'London Omnibus Company Limited' by the French company's opponents who proclaimed that they would be an Eng-

lish firm running English omnibuses built by English coachbuilders. Nothing came of the London Omnibus Company but it succeeded, indirectly, by putting 'General' into the successful company's title, in giving it the name by which it came to be best known – 'the General'.

The competition excited a good deal of interest and the judges found themselves with 75 entries to inspect. The judges were George Godwin, editor of *The Builder* (which, it will be recalled, was the first to call for the conversion of London to the Parisian mode), Charles Manby, Secretary of the Institution of Civil Engineers, and Joseph Wright, a prominent builder of railway rolling stock. They were not greatly enamoured of any single design though they admitted that several showed considerable ingenuity and offered some improvements. They awarded the £100 to R. F. Miller of Hammersmith because, though they could not recommend the adoption of his design as it stood, it seemed to them to contain the most detailed improvements and to be the best suited for development.

The modified Miller omnibus became the standard knifeboard type of the L.G.O.C. Its main advantages included better headroom inside – most people had had to crouch before but were now given a full 6ft. – and greater width. There was room for 12 passengers inside. Ventilation was also improved by a clerestory roof which originally gave seats for passengers on the offside only but was soon modified to have 'knifeboard' type seats on both sides. Passengers reached the roof by a series of metal plates instead of the usual rungs and one of these plates, rather larger than the others and popularly known as the 'monkey board', formed the conductor's platform. Handholds were also provided for use in reaching the roof which seated 10 on the knifeboard and two on each side of the driver. The conductor had a strap on which to hang to avoid falling off his step – it was also convenient for lowering himself to the ground at stops and for swinging back on to his step afterwards. An attempt at introducing a mechanical call system so that passengers could indicate where they wanted to alight came to nothing and in the end conductors were issued with whistles to signal to the driver. How one gained the attention of the conductor is not known – presumably shouts or even prods as in the earlier days. These improved buses were slow to appear at first, but there were nearly 250 by the end of 1858.

two doors facing the rear, one on each side, with the conductor's step in between with step-plates and handrails leading to the roof, which had a longitudinal central well. Roof passengers sat facing each other on seats along both sides of the roof with their feet in the well. A version of this omnibus was used by the Metropolitan Saloon Omnibus Co. Ltd., which built about 15 of these vehicles and competed with the L.G.O.C. for just over two years, from April 1857 to July 1859.

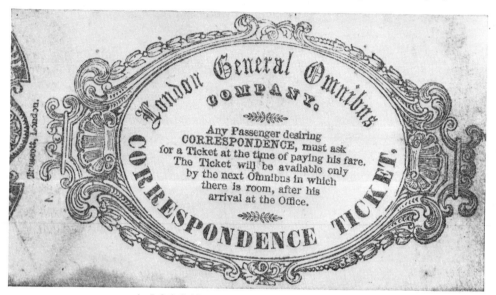

An L.G.O.C. 'Correspondence' or transfer ticket of 1856

The design of a new omnibus was not an easy task. Experience had shown that if the vehicle weighed more than 21cwt. it was too much for two horses (and there were no brakes), and that if the width between the wheels was much more than 6ft. – 6ft. 6in. was the absolute limit – the vehicle could not be manoevred. It should be remembered that, as with all horse-drawn vehicles of the period, the body of the omnibus sat *between* the wheels, so that the width of the body was limited by the width of the wheeltrack and the need for the front wheels to swivel. One ingenious design submitted, by T. B. Ashford, was for a so-called 'saloon' omnibus. It had

The L.G.O.C. introduced some buses from outside London to fill the gap until its own new buses were built, in particular some three-horse buses of a type used in Birmingham and Glasgow. These carried 17 passengers inside and 25 on the roof where they sat back-to-back with the clerestory roof as a seat back between them. This meant that everyone's legs dangled over the edge of the roof, so a special footboard was placed along each side, half-way up the saloon windows, to take the rows of feet. There were also cross-seats on the roof, taking two on each side of the driver and five on a seat behind him. Getting to one's seat must have entailed considerable athleticism – as it must have done on almost any omnibus of the period.

As well as bringing in buses from outside, the L.G.O.C. made improvements to over 200 of its existing buses, raising the roof to give more headroom inside and improving access to the roof. Despite all this, the company was still very worried about the state of its fleet at the end of 1858 and doubted whether some of its buses would be able to pass the police inspection.

ticket – and sometimes at no extra cost. Paris could use the system easily because so much of the city was confined within the lines of the old walls and it formed a compact entity, but in sprawling London the problem was very different. In Paris a 3d. ticket covered two omnibus routes and in practice almost any point in the city to any other.

The *correspondence* system in London began in April 1856 with allowing passengers from Barnet on what might be called a

Knifeboard bus at Peckham, 1864

In Paris, the *correspondence* system had found great favour with passengers and the *Conseil* was anxious that it should be brought into use in London. To the London managers this was an alien concept for which they appear to have had no enthusiasm, but try it they did. In any case the system had been much publicized and praised during the formation of the company. The *correspondence* system was in effect a system of issuing transfer tickets so that passengers could transfer from one route to another without having to buy an extra

'trunk' route to the suburbs to change at specified points to other routes to reach various points in central London. No extra charge was made for this facility. The next stage was the opening of offices at correspondence points where passengers had to have their tickets stamped before transferring to another route. The system gained some popularity among travellers at other than peak times but its use slowly fell away and at the end of 1858 it was abandoned.

There were constant urgings from Paris

that the company should take over the remainder of the London omnibuses, of which 210 were still in other hands, and Foucaud, supported by Edwin Chadwick, prepared a plan which would have brought all the buses, the river steamers, and any tramways (Paris saw its first line in 1853) into a single co-ordinated relationship. The L.G.O.C. actually subscribed, much against the London managers' wishes, £10,000 towards buying up some of the Thames steamers, but the scheme fell through – no doubt to their great relief. As regards the 210 buses, the managers had no desire to take them over. They established relationships with the associations which ran the other buses, sometimes by buying their way in, and agreed routes and times with them. Among well-known names in these associations was Mrs. Birch (afterwards Birch Bros.) and Thomas Tilling – the latter one of those who refused to come to terms with the L.G.O.C. but was willing to co-operate in working practices. For example, he took part in the *correspondence* ticket scheme.

Paris also urged the speedy introduction of tramways into London and the L.G.O.C. set up a company, the London Omnibus Tramway Company, late in 1857. The tracks would have run from the Bank via Moorgate, the City Road and the New Road to Bayswater and Notting Hill Gate. At King's Cross a branch line would have turned off down Farringdon Street to Fleet Street. The Chief Commissioner of Public Works (Sir Benjamin Hall, after whom 'Big Ben' is named) was strongly opposed to the scheme and the Parliamentary Bill to give powers to lay the track was defeated on second reading.

As will be gathered, remote control through the Paris *Conseil* was proving something of a trial to the London managers. Another instruction was to fit counting devices (which had been tried earlier, it will be recalled) to all omnibuses to check the conductor's takings. This was given a token trial and declared unsatisfactory. It was usual at that time to watch the takings of each bus and if a conductor turned in, regularly, an amount consistently lower than that produced by others on the route, he was watched by a road inspector. The managers considered this more effective than indicators.

However, one scheme which *was* introduced was the sale of vouchers which at any time could be used to pay fares. If vouchers to the value of one pound were purchased at any one time, the purchaser was entitled to a discount of 10 per cent. These lasted from 1857 to 1859, and large stores seem to have given some of them away as a bonus to their customers. (Something similar has been done in some American cities in recent times.)

It may be useful at this point to give some idea of the extent of the services run by the L.G.O.C., though it is no purpose of this book – indeed it is far too small – to discuss the build-up and extent of individual routes. As we have seen, the company took over 600 buses and these operated at the time 50 routes. By April 1857, 33 of these buses were taken out of service and held in reserve, but the number of routes (or 'lines' as they were then called) had increased to 63, though they covered more or less the same ground as the original 50. On an average day in the first year of operation, 450 buses were actually in service, and each bus ran 54 miles, giving a total of 24,000 bus-miles daily. Each horse – there were 5,879 – worked 12 miles a day and was fed on 16 lb. of bruised oats and 10 lb. of a mixture of hay and straw. Routes ran along most roads between the centre and the edges of built-up London with others to such points as Stratford, Merton, and Croydon, Kilburn, Wimbledon, and Putney. A curious addition was the four-horse mail service between the G.P.O. in London and Barnet, and a similar service to Woodford. The mail buses also carried passengers.

At one time it was possible to pre-book a seat on a regularly-used omnibus on a weekly basis – or longer – but this must have caused many complications when a 'regular' failed to arrive to take his place, or, worse, arrived late after the conductor had already decided he was not coming and had given the place to another passenger. A form of bell was introduced so that the passenger could let the conductor (not the driver) know he wished to alight. The conductor then, presumably, signalled to the driver with his whistle.

The L.G.O.C. paid a 12½ per cent. dividend on the first year's working, a figure somewhat less than some of the estimates but certainly one that would be welcomed today. The average earnings of a bus were £2.19s. 6½d. a day and the biggest item of costs, the upkeep of the horses, took £1.8s. 1d. a day. Wages took only 9s. 9d. a day; vehicle upkeep took 4s. 3½d.; administrative and other general expenses took 3s. 11½d.; licences, tolls, and duties took 6s. 7d.; and accidents and inspections accounted for 9½d. a day. The remaining 6s. 1d. was profit. Some of the steps taken to improve profits by cutting costs and tighter administration have already been described. The Highbury depot, which, as already mentioned, took over the maintenance of the omnibuses and the building of a number of new ones, proved capable of looking after three-quarters of the fleet at an average cost of 15s. a vehicle per week or 2s. 6d. less than the price charged by the contractors who maintained the rest of the vehicles. Another economy was the reduction of the original 10 administrative districts to six – Brompton, Eastern and Southern, Hackney, Highbury, Paddington, and St. John's Wood – saving about £1,750 a year in administrative expenses. A further saving was achieved by moving the head offices from 454 West Strand to cheaper premises, costing £300 a year less, at 31 Moorgate.

The wages of the crew were deducted, by the conductor, from the day's takings before he handed them in, and he paid the driver and himself. At the beginning he also paid any tolls from the takings. Although this sounds a strange practice, it was in keeping with the customs of the times and the L.G.O.C. was in many ways a model employer. For example, it offered continuity of work to employees in an unsettled time and proposed to set up a provident fund for them, paying in sums itself in proportion to those paid by the employees. The scheme was dropped because very few of the crews themselves showed any enthusiasm for it – they may have been suspicious since hardly anything of the sort existed elsewhere at the time.

In 1857 there were some 2,300 staff and already a million passengers a week were being carried by L.G.O.C. omnibuses. Turnpike tolls even then worked out at a total of £18,000 a year and the mileage duty at £48,000. By comparison, the licensing duty paid for the year, at £2,000, was negligible.

Competition appeared for the moment to have died down under the various agreements, but it began again in 1857–58 with adventures by mostly small companies which appeared and vanished quickly but caused the L.G.O.C. a great deal of trouble while they lasted. The L.G.O.C.'s weapons were more buses and lower fares on the routes where the rivals appeared, but this policy, though effective, cut into the company's profits. Another practice was to hem in the upstart vehicle with L.G.O.C. omnibuses so that it could not collect passengers or stop where it wanted. This particular method of fighting competition also resulted in fights among the crews and police court cases followed. In fairness to the L.G.O.C. (and the Associations, which used similar methods against the newcomers) it should be pointed out that they had been allotted, or had spent considerable sums in purchasing 'times', and their routes were run in a regular and orderly fashion to a high standard. The newcomers did none of these things, seeking only to take profit at times when there were plenty of passengers and vanishing after the traffic peaks. This phase died out in the mid-1860s but 'piracy', as it came to be called, was to raise its head (or the 'Jolly Roger') again in London's bus history.

One example from this early period may be of interest, since the rival was the Metropolitan Saloon Omnibus Company mentioned earlier. (This company presented a petition in bankruptcy in April 1858.) The police had suggested that the case between the two companies should be put to arbitration and the parties appeared to state their cases at Westminster Police Court (this was in 1858). The Metropolitan Saloon Omnibus Company accused the L.G.O.C. of a conspiracy, the object of which was to 'injure, libel, and ruin' its rival. A Metropolitan omnibus was stated to have been hemmed in by five L.G.O.C. buses, one of which, it was claimed, had driven up close behind the Metropolitan bus so that the pole between its horses pressed hard on the door of the Metropolitan omnibus and prevented anyone from getting in or out. The L.G.O.C. was also accused of 'publishing a libellous imputation of insolvency'. The L.G.O.C. denied the hustling, or 'nursing' as it was called at the time, of the Metropolitan omnibus and implied that the Metropolitan company had been formed only to make a nuisance of itself to the L.G.O.C. in the hope that the L.G.O.C. would buy it out. (The policy of the L.G.O.C. in fact was to let the companies fail, on the principle that to buy out one would only cause a shoal of other companies to be formed for the very purpose of being bought out.) It was not until 1862 that the arbitrator finally found for the L.G.O.C. and announced that all the Metropolitan Saloon company's charges had failed.

The fall in profits due to the need to fight competition brought the matter of control from France to a crisis. The French shareholders, and therefore the French members of the *Conseil*, were not happy at the turn of events and the English members of the *Conseil* supported the managers in London in their opinion that the company should be an English one with control in London and that company meetings should be held in London. Even Chadwick supported this view, but the French members would have nothing of it, declaring that if only French methods were brought in all would be well. A further fall in profits, plus well-timed reports from London that they were being accused of being agents of a foreign power and running a foreign monopoly, and that this was being held against them in the courts and in public and political opinion, made the French shareholders think again. On 1 January 1859 the undertaking became officially, instead of just by translation, the London General Omnibus Company Ltd. The financial side of the transfer was accomplished by an exchange of shares, the nominal capital being £800,000. The number of French directors and French shareholders fell slowly over the years but the annual report continued to be printed in French as well as English right up to 1911. In practice, French influence faded out of the picture during the Franco-Prussian War of 1870.

IV The Years of Development

THE new company had a far from clean start. The directors found the L.G.O.C. was more than £100,000 in debt, suggesting that the French shareholders had been more interested in dividends than in ploughing back money for improvements, financing new developments by borrowing instead of from revenue. The new chairman of the company was William Halliday Cosway, who had for 1859 whereas £18,000 of the previous year's profit had gone in this way. At the end of 1859 there were 78 buses running in opposition, some having been withdrawn when the L.G.O.C. became an English company, but the number began to rise again. The number of passengers also began to climb – from nearly 39 million in 1859 to 41.4 million in 1861. In 1862 there was a great exhibition

---

LONDON GENERAL OMNIBUS CO., LIMITED.

OMNIBUS PARCELS DESPATCH.

The advantages offered by the above Service are

FREQUENT DELIVERIES DAILY

To all parts of London and the Suburbs, and lower charges than those of any other Company.

RATES, INCLUDING COLLECTION AND DELIVERY.

Not exceeding 1 lb. (prepaid)	. . . . .	2d.
Over 1 lb. and not exceeding 4 lbs.	. . .	3d.
„ 4 lbs. „ „ 7 „	. . .	4d.
„ 7 „ „ „ 14 „	. . .	6d.
„ 14 „ „ „ 28 „	. . .	8d.

Large Millinery Boxes no less charge than 6d.
NO CHARGE FOR BOOKING.

Receiving Offices at short distances from each other are upon each Omnibus route, and parcels (not prepaid) may be handed to any of the Company's Conductors on their journey.
Contracts, by which a considerable saving may be effected, entered into with houses sending out a considerable number of Parcels.

Further information afforded on application to Mr. W. H. SOLLAS, Agent for this Service, at the

Central Office, No. 144, CHEAPSIDE.

⁂ It is particularly requested that any instance of refusal by a Conductor to receive a Parcel be communicated, with the number of the Omnibus, to the Central Office, as above.

---

become a member of the London *Conseil* towards the end of 1857, but the main task of pulling the company together descended on McNamara, advised by the other former London manager, Willing, and the district managers.

The profit for 1859 was £24,046 against £23,888 for 1858, but no dividend was paid in London and once again passengers flocked to the omnibuses. The L.G.O.C. did well, earning £72,503, much of which was used to reduce the opening debt to £64,000.

In 1863 came the opening of the first section of the Metropolitan Railway, from Paddington to Farringdon Street, and with it opened a new era of competition for London's omnibuses. The tale of the expansion of the Underground is told in *The Story of London's Underground* (also published by London Transport) so in this book it will be referred to only as it affected the omnibuses. The main effect was, in fact, to restrict the growth of traffic – though it continued to grow steadily – and to restrict the growth of profits, which fell steadily.

The fall in profits despite increased traffic reflected the need to reduce fares to compete with the new railways where they offered a competitive service, although the L.G.O.C. showed some ingenuity in developing new routes, free from competition, where there

to go to the railways, but where journeys were short and the destination was more conveniently reached by omnibus, the omnibuses gained the traffic. The pattern of shorter journeys by bus and longer ones by rail – particularly where a bus can be boarded in the main street whereas some effort may have to be made via subways, steps, or escalators, or lifts, to reach a station ticket office and then the platform – still persists today. In the 1860s, however, the West End in particular had no railways and the omnibus was king.

The *London Omnibus Guide* of 1866 casts some interesting lights on this period. For example, there was apparently an active

THE

LONDON OMNIBUS GUIDE,

AND

Local Conveyance Directory.

1866.

NOTES FOR OMNIBUS RIDERS.

THE fares given in this Guide, and written on the inside of the doors of the Omnibuses, are those for the conveyance of the passengers only, *without luggage*, which must be paid for extra. A small bag, box, or parcel, of such a size as not to cause any inconvenience to the passengers, it is, however, not usual to charge for.

Baskets of fish or bulky packages are not permitted inside an Omnibus.

Dogs, when objected to by the passengers, are not to be admitted inside the vehicle.

Children, *occupying seats*, must be paid for at the same rate as adult passengers.

Property found in an Omnibus must be immediately handed over to the Conductor, whose duty it is to deliver the same at the nearest police-station, whence it is forwarded to the Lost Property Office, Scotland Yard, where all inquiries in reference to missing articles should be made.

On several lines of route it will be found that the fares are increased after 8 p.m. on Sundays. The fare is charged according to the time at which the passenger alights from the Omnibus; thus, if a passenger enters the Omnibus at 7.30 p.m., and alights at 8.5 p.m., the increased fare is chargeable.

If it be found necessary to communicate with the Proprietor of an Omnibus on any subject, his name and address may be ascertained on application at the Metropolitan Stage Carriage Office, Somerset House, giving the plate number of the vehicle as a means of identification.

Seats in an Omnibus may be engaged by the week or otherwise, *by prepayment only*. It is not lawful for a Conductor to retain a seat for any rider unless the fare be prepaid.

was an untapped traffic potential. This could only go so far, however, and omnibus traffic ceased to grow while that of the railways rapidly expanded. The shape of London passenger traffic began to emerge and the L.G.O.C. recognized, in a statement made in 1870, that, where railways and omnibuses were in competition, through traffic tended

L.G.O.C. parcels traffic, for an advertisement appears in the *Guide* (*left*).

Even more interesting are the introductory notes for all omnibus riders (*above*).

On 18 January 1867, McNamara died and his place as General Manager of the L.G.O.C. was taken by Augustus George Church, who had been Secretary since the first days of the

French company. He continued to act also as Secretary and eventually, in 1879, was given a seat on the board. Also in 1867 came the Metropolitan Streets Act, which at first applied to the City and to an area which subsequently became the County of London. The Act, which came into force on November 1, contained provisions obliging omnibuses to pick up and set down traffic on the near side of the road instead of wandering from one side to the other as passengers required. This applied at first to an area within four miles of Charing Cross but was extended to six miles in 1885. One of the great bones of contention, the mileage payment, was reduced from 1d. a mile to $\frac{1}{4}$d. a mile on 2 July 1866. This disliked duty, which the busmen thought bore very unfairly on them and had been taking about 9 per cent. of their receipts, was abolished altogether from the end of 1869 and tolls, too, were first reduced and then removed altogether in the 1860s.

The Metropolitan Public Carriage Act of 1869 put all licensing powers in the hands of the Commissioner of Police and in the first year of operation of the Act, 1870, he seems to have used these powers to some effect in securing the removal of quite a number of dilapidated vehicles from the roads. The L.G.O.C. fleet remained fairly static, but in 1862 twenty-three horse buses which had been introduced by the Manchester company, Greenwood & Turner, to reap the harvest of the great exhibition traffic of that year, were sold at low prices to the L.G.O.C. rather than incur the considerable cost of taking them all back to Manchester when the exhibition ended. In November 1865, the omnibuses and the routes of the Richmond Conveyance Company, which had been operating since 1844, were acquired for £4,900 on the ending of the 21-year agreement between the companies. The Metropolitan, and later the Metropolitan District, railways were anxious that the L.G.O.C. should provide feeder bus services to their stations and the Metropolitan asked the L.G.O.C. to provide such services when it opened in 1863. In August 1866 the

Metropolitan began to run its own buses between what is now Great Portland Street Station and Oxford Circus, extending the route in 1874 to Piccadilly. Another Metropolitan service, started in 1872, linked Camden Town with the present Euston Square Station. This second service ended in 1874. When the Metropolitan District began operations it subsidized an L.G.O.C. service on the Paddington–Park Lane–Victoria route. The subsidy was needed for some years but the route eventually became self-supporting and finally very profitable so that the subsidy could be withdrawn.

To go back a little, it is interesting to note the fares which were being charged for omnibus journeys in London in the 1860s. Here are some taken from the July 1866 fare tables (after the abolition of the turnpikes and their tolls):

Charing Cross–Westminster Abbey......2d.
Elephant & Castle–Kennington ....2d.
King's Cross–Holborn.................2d.
Euston Road–Oxford Street............2d.
Westminster–Temple Bar (Fleet Street)..3d.
Victoria Station–Marble Arch..........3d.
Hampstead–Camden Town ....4d.
Highgate Hill–Charing Cross..........6d.

On the in-Town routes the maximum fare was usually 6d. and the minimum 2d., but on Sunday evenings after 18 00 the charge was 6d. for any distance. There was one odd exception on the Hammersmith–Bank route where, after 20 00 on Sundays, the outside fare was 6d. but the passenger who wanted to sit inside had to pay 9d. Some of the longer distance routes had higher fares. For example, the trip from Finchley into central London cost 1s., as it did from Woodford or Brentford. The Colnbrook–London trip seems to have been the most expensive at 2s. 6d., though this was reduced to 2s. for outside travellers – the only route, apart from the Sunday evening one just mentioned, on which such a reduction seems to have applied. There was one, and only one, penny fare – between Highbury Station and Highbury

Barn. In this year of 1866 the L.G.O.C. made a profit of £37,479.

In 1866 also, the L.G.O.C. made its first stand against the rigours of the English climate. This was not by protecting its passengers but by starting to buy imported maize to avoid the variations in the price of oats used for feeding the horses. The price of oats could vary so much between good and bad British harvests that the extra costs could swallow up the entire profit for the year – and more. The year 1866 saw also the first fatal accident, when a passenger fell from one of the buses. When one considers the primitive means of access to the roof – and the not much better way into the interior – used by people of all ages and conditions, it is amazing that the L.G.O.C. could have operated for ten years, carrying hundreds of millions of passengers, before this first fatality. The company paid a substantial sum in compensation to the widow of the victim.

The administration of the company seems to have been very good, and falling receipts were met by economies in operation. After the disastrous year of 1867, when the L.G.O.C. incurred a deficit of £2,833, things looked much brighter, though there could be considerable fluctuations in annual results. There were other sources of income than fares, though these were obviously not of such great import. One was the letting of advertising rights on the omnibuses – a contract held by James Willing (still a name in advertising) until 1859 – and still a source of considerable revenue to London Transport today. Another source of income, which has *not* survived, was the sale of horse manure. The directors were not slow to examine the possibilities of new routes where there were prospects of new traffic, and suggestions from passengers were always carefully examined.

The effect of a bad summer on the price of horse fodder has been noted, but the converse was also true. A good summer might bring lower prices for fodder but it also brought sickness to the horses. The veterinary service maintained by the L.G.O.C. was a

very good one and the care of the horses was something of importance to the directors, who considered reports of sickness and death among the horses at every board meeting. The horses at this time worked for three hours a day, and new premises were acquired for stables as routes were changed or extended so that the horses did not have too far to go before and after their spells of duty. Although the horses worked only for three hours and

A typical horse bus driver and conductor in 1875. The driver, William Parragreen, was nicknamed 'Cast-Iron Billy'. Originally a cab driver, he drove omnibuses from 1834 and worked for the L.G.O.C.

drew their omnibus not more than 15 miles in that time, the crews stayed with their vehicles from the first journey in the morning until the last at night – a day which could easily stretch to 16 hours.

Two more small sources of income were the parcels service for some five years in the 1860s which was not as flourishing as the advertisement already quoted made it appear, and

[27]

was consequently dropped; and a private hire service which still exists today. The revenue from this varied from a few hundred pounds a year to a few thousand until the end of 1869, when a considerable fall after the end of the contract (inherited from the company's predecessors) for carrying prisoners suggested that this had been one of the mainstays of private hire down to that time.

We might close this section with a quotation from an 1874 journal, which said:

'The efficiency of the service of the London General Omnibus Company is proverbial, while the attention at all times given to the complaints of passengers as well as to the interests of the Company, by its active Secretary, Mr. Augustus George Church, is admitted at once, and while every route in London is so admirably served, indeed, that it is next to an impossibility not to travel from anywhere to everywhere either in London or its suburbs, without comfort or rapidity.'

Early in the 1870s came new source of income, bitter-sweet though it must have been, with the gaining of contracts for horsing the new rival of the omnibus – the horse tram. Horses were provided at a flat rate per mile, and by 1875 this service was earning £50,000 a year.

The coming of the tram had other effects, however, on the maintenance of the omnibuses, as this extract from *Design and Work* of 2 March 1878 shows. It is given in full for its general interest:

'THE LONDON GENERAL OMNIBUS COMPANY. – In the recently-issued half-yearly report of this company, as usual, interesting statistics are given, from which we find that the number of passengers carried in the six months was 26,611,280, by 580 omnibuses working on weekdays, and 494 on Sundays, at an average fare per passenger of 2½d. The ordinary omnibus traffic has produced £1,180 more than in the corresponding period in 1876, horsing tramway cars £1,684 more, but the sale of manure and advertising brought in £135 less. The number of horses on the 31st December was 7972, and the quantity of grain consumed was 5007 qrs. of oats, 47,988 qrs. of maize, and 773 qrs. of beans. Reference is made to the increased charge for the maintenance of rolling stock, which is attributed to the defective condition in some districts of the tramways, and it is stated that the cost of the wheels has increased since the introduction of the latter from £9.10s. per annum per omnibus to £15. "It is understood that the Board of Trade have taken the matter in hand, and possibly some material improvement will result from the interference of that department." '

This last theme was still evident the following year, when the directors expressed their astonishment that the authorities 'who professedly have charge of the streets of the Metropolis' allowed the roads used by the tramways to remain in a condition which was 'so highly dangerous to the public, and so seriously destructive to all ordinary wheeled vehicles'.

It should not be thought that the L.G.O.C. was itself indifferent to tramways. As we have seen in an earlier chapter, promptings from Paris had caused the L.G.O.C. to launch the London Omnibus Tramway Co. Ltd. in 1857. The efficiency of wheels on rails, instead of the ordinary road surface, was such that two horses could haul at least twice the weight. The L.O.T.C. itself would have had two-ton trams which would have carried 60 passengers each. Comparison with the standard bus load of the time shows that the horses would have been used to three times the effect – and the provision of horses was the greatest expense in the L.G.O.C. accounts.

Although the L.G.O.C. failed in its attempts to introduce tramways to London their success in America made it certain that they would arrive before long. The bastions of Paris had fallen to the tramway in 1853 when a line was opened from the Place de la Concorde to Passy. Extended to Sèvres the following year, this line with its 40-seat cars became part of the official Paris transport system in 1855. What Paris did then, London did the next day, and the *Chemin de Fer Américain* caused great interest. When an American tramway expert, George Francis Train, arrived in London with proposals for a tramway there were many willing to listen. Marylebone argued hotly about a proposed Train line which would have taken in Oxford Street, Wigmore Street, and Baker Street in the course of its career via Gloucester Place from Finchley Road and back. The Vestry may have been swayed against the proposals by the strong objections of the L.G.O.C., but probably the character of the streets chosen by Train was as much to do with this particular failure as anything.

Train had more success with a more modest trial line from Marble Arch along the Bayswater Road as far as Porchester Terrace and another along Victoria Street from Westminster Abbey. These two lines, known respectively as the Marble Arch Street Railway and the Westminster Street Railway, were both opened in 1861, the first on March 23 and the second on April 15. A third short line from the eastern end of Westminster Bridge to Kennington Gate, known as the Surrey Side Street Railway, opened on 15 August. The first passenger on Train's first tramway is said to have been George Cruikshank, the artist.

These lines demonstrated quite conclusively the advantages of the street tramway to its passengers and operators. Train himself declared that he could not think that 'anyone would wish to throw any impediment in the way of introducing so great a luxury as the people's carriage'. Others were not so happy. Although rails which lay flush with the roadway were already available and had been used with success in America, Train chose to lay the type of rail, the 'step rail', with which he was familiar from his experience in Philadelphia. These rails needed expert laying if they were not to protrude from the road surface, and this was lacking. Complaints were many, and after a few months Train's lines were closed down. It is said that these abortive attempts to introduce tramways were the main reason why tramways were never allowed nearer than the fringe of the West End, though fears of their causing street congestion seem equally likely to have been the reason long after objections to Train's tramways – and the manner of his personal advocacy of them – had faded into history.

Advocacy of tramways continued, however, and the sanction by Parliament of a tramway in Liverpool in 1868 emboldened promoters. In 1869 three London schemes were put before Parliament and approved after, among other things, assurances had been given that the type of rail used would in no way interfere with other road traffic. The L.G.O.C., which had been opposing tramways for the past few years and enlisting support against them, hurriedly changed its tune and contracted with one of the new tramways, the North Metropolitan, to provide horses for its trams, beginning the lucrative association already noted. The North Metropolitan provided a service along the Whitechapel, Mile End, and Bow roads. The other two companies were the Metropolitan Street Tramways along the Train pioneer route from Westminster Bridge to Kennington and on to Brixton and Clapham, and the Pimlico, Peckham & Greenwich Tramway between Vauxhall and Greenwich. These two companies joined together as the London Tramways Company soon after they began operations in 1870. Another company, the London Street Tramways Company, began operations in St. Pancras and Kentish Town the following year.

The new tramways attracted a great deal of traffic right from the start, with the North Metropolitan company, for example, topping the million mark in its first six months. The passing of the Tramways Act in 1870 – after some skirmishing over who had and had not the power to permit or veto the building of tramways in the London streets – brought many new schemes into being. The Metropolitan Board of Works, which had managed to establish itself as the tramway authority –

though unable to impose its decisions on the street authorities who held powers of veto – considered plans for over 100 miles of tramway in 1871. One of its rules was that applications for routes on which there was not already a well-patronized omnibus service would be refused on the grounds that there was no suitable traffic potential. Another was that a route between the suburbs and the centre was to be run entirely, throughout its length, by a single company. The Metropolitan Board of Works saw no objection to tramways in the centre of London, but its support for proposals of this type really brought out the opposition and in 1872 Parliament decided that the centre of London should be forbidden to tramways. The City, also, held out against tramways, mainly on the grounds that the City streets were unsuitable for this type of transport.

We cannot follow the story of the trams in detail, for this is the story of the omnibus, but it seems true that quite early the tram (which issued workmen's tickets from the 1870s while the bus did not) became the working-class conveyance just as the bus had long been that of the middle class. Passenger traffic in London grew as the city itself grew, and the buses and trams flourished side by side. The North Metropolitan, by 1876, had extended its original $9\frac{1}{2}$ miles of line to 30 miles and was carrying 27 million passengers a year. It was still getting its horses under contract from the L.G.O.C., which was getting $6\frac{3}{4}$d. for every car-mile the tramway worked – and in 1876 that was more than 3.5 million. Each tramcar needed a stud of 11 horses to meet its full day's working, and the working life of a tram-horse at the time was about four years.

In 1875, the year before this, bus and tram traffic had almost reached parity, with the trams carrying 48.9 million and the buses 49.7 million.

The failure of the trams to win the right to enter central London seems to have been the salvation of the omnibus since it retained the lucrative West End and City traffic. It also retained some traffic along the tram routes leading to the centre, for no-one wanted to have to change from tram to bus at the edge of central London unless there was a considerable financial inducement. As the tram fares were much lower than those of the buses, to prevent the financial inducement being given the omnibus fares along the tram routes had to be substantially reduced – which was a very good thing for Londoners if not for the shareholders of the L.G.O.C. and other bus undertakings.

V Competition and Expansion

THE provision of horses for the tramways brought the L.G.O.C. a steady income up to 1878 and as soon as this contract ended the company introduced nearly 50 extra buses which were to be worked by the best of the former tramway horses. Receipts, which had declined in 1879, began to rise again and by 1880 were back to the £90,000 figure of 1878. The prosperity of the L.G.O.C. and other providers of road transport in London

successful at raising money, and it was not until March 1881 that any real advance was made with the display of four new buses before they went into service. One of the buses was of conventional design, with detail improvements, but the other three were designed by Captain Molesworth, of the Royal Navy, and were quite unusual. With the success of the tramway loading platforms in mind the bus had very small wheels at the

Oxford Circus in 1888, with 'knifeboard' and 'garden seat' buses

had not gone un-noticed. A London business association, interested in promoting companies to enter any kind of business which promised reasonable returns, in 1878 took a look at the state of things in London and sent its agents to examine the state of road passenger traffic in Europe (including, naturally enough, Paris). On 3 August 1880 there was formed, as a result, the London & District Omnibus Co. Ltd.

The new company was not, in fact, very

front with an entry platform above them. Stairways ran from each side of the platform up to top deck level and behind the stairs a door opened into the lower saloon, which had upholstered seats. An innovation on the top deck was the provision of what came to be known as 'garden seats' which faced the direction of travel instead of running back-to-back down the centre of the roof.

Attractive as these buses were, it was soon realized that any passenger who slipped on

'Garden seat' bus belonging to the London Road-Car Company seen at West Kensington in 1894. Note the Union Jack trademark at the masthead on the offside front

alighting was only too well positioned to be run over by the rear wheels. With this in mind the body was reversed, bringing the low platform to the rear. In this form the buses were even more like the trams which had inspired them and became very popular. Taking advantage of the tram likeness, the company changed its name in April 1881 to the London Road-Car Company. Its first buses, drawn by three horses, began to run between Victoria and Hammersmith, flying a Union Jack on each bus as a reminder to all and sundry of the French origins of the L.G.O.C. A new route began to work in the opposite direction from Victoria to Broad Street. Between them these two routes covered most of what is now Route 11. Another route, between Victoria and Oxford Circus, was soon added, but the fortunes of the London Road-Car Company

were not auspicious. After a very shaky start, with changes on the board of directors and even liquidation and re-formation under the same name in 1882, things slowly improved and at the beginning of the 1890s it had about 240 buses and assets approaching £230,000. At this time (1890) the company was carrying 37 million passengers a year.

In the same year the L.G.O.C. carried 112 million passengers. Shaken by the new competition – not only from the London Road-Car Company – the L.G.O.C. had reduced fares and put on extra buses, bringing the fleet by 1891 to 891, with its associated proprietors operating a further 202 buses. The total opposition bus fleet amounted to 595, but there were also 847 tramcars. Fortunately, there was traffic for all. Helped no doubt by the cheaper fares induced by commercial rivalry and the demand for in-town bus and tram journeys brought about by the cheaper travel to London provided by the main line railway companies, the growth of traffic was enormous. The tramways, for example, saw their traffic increase threefold from 65 million in 1880 to 189 million in 1890.

The non-L.G.O.C. buses, apart from those run by its allies, were operated by various companies. They included those of the Metropolitan Railway, mentioned earlier (Chapter IV), which in 1883 were extended from Piccadilly to Charing Cross. This extension continued in operation for nearly 10 years. Five years later, in 1888, the Metropolitan began a service between Baker Street and Piccadilly Circus via Oxford Street and Bond Street, and in 1892 the railway began another service. This ran from Edgware Road Station via Edgware Road, Oxford Street, and Tottenham Court Road to Gower Street Station (now Euston Square). Like the other Metropolitan buses, it carried a large red umbrella to protect the driver from the elements. The Metropolitan conductors, or 'guards', wore a uniform – unusual, to say the least, for busmen at this period. The original Metropolitan buses had three horses, but by this time some two-thirds of the vehicles were drawn, like most London omnibuses, by two horses only. Other rivals in this period included the London Omnibus-Carriage Company, with about 40 buses; Thomas Tilling (though only a handful of that firm's buses were actually rivals of the L.G.O.C. vehicles); the 'Star' (Andrews' Star Omnibus Company), also with some 40 buses; and the Railways & Metropolitan Omnibus Company with just over 20 buses. Apart from these, there were many small proprietors with a handful of buses each.

The speed of buses in London at this time, including stops, worked out at an average of about 5 m.p.h. at fares averaging just under a penny a mile. Most routes had four or five buses an hour, though there were busier ones with up to 15 an hour.

The table below, first published in *London General** and compiled from an 1888 copy of Bennett's *Intelligence Quarterly*, gives a representative collection of routes and frequencies:

FROM	To	MILES	JOURNEY TIMES (Mins.)	FREQUENCY (Mins.)	FARE
	LONDON HORSE-BUS SERVICES 1888				
Hammersmith	Liverpool Street	7	70	4	4d.
Liverpool Street	Victoria	3½	40	4	2d.
St. John's Wood	London Bridge	5¾	56	8	6d.
Royal Oak	London Bridge	5½	56	4	5d.
Charing Cross	Kilburn	4½	50	12	4d.
Cricklewood	Oxford Circus	4½	48	30	5d.
Liverpool Street	Ladbroke Grove	6	70	10	5d.
Putney	London Bridge	7½	80	15	6d.
Elephant & Castle	Kingsland	3½	40	7	3d.
Harlesden	Charing Cross	7½	75	60	6d.
West Kilburn	London Bridge	6	69	12	6d.
King's Cross	Waterloo	2½	25	12	3d.

The L.G.O.C. was slow to adopt some of the improvements introduced by the Road-Car Company, particularly the popular 'garden seats'. One reason given was that many of the buses were too old to be adapted in this way – which suggests that the proportion of modern vehicles was not very high. It was only too clear to the shareholders that, although their own traffic was growing as the popular demand for services increased, the traffic carried by the Road-Car Company, not much more than a quarter the size of the L.G.O.C., was growing not at an equal rate but in very nearly equal *numbers* of passengers. Something had to be done.

In 1891 A. G. Church, who for 36 years had served the L.G.O.C. as Secretary, General Manager, and Managing Director, retired on grounds of ill-health and age. His place was taken by R. G. Hall and it was not long before the L.G.O.C. began to cast around for a method of making sure that the money paid by passengers actually found its way into the hands of the company. The chairman of the company, ten years or more earlier, had told shareholders how he had boarded a bus to find only two passengers marked on the con-

* Published by London Transport in 1956; now out of print.

ductor's sheet. When taxed with the discrepancy, he put down another two passengers. Pressed further, he added another four and eventually another two. With the same system still in force, it was no wonder that the L.G.O.C. had cause for concern. In his time, Church had relied on spot checks by agents, not known to the conductors, who rode on the buses and reported on what they found – today they might be described as 'plain clothes inspectors'.

The original contract tickets of the early 1850s were soon discontinued and it was not until 1877 that the L.G.O.C. became suffi-

introduction of a single flat fare or of a bonus on receipts.

The Road-Car Company was using a roll ticket system and paying royalties to the Bell Punch Company at least by 1885. This system was later simplified so that numbered but unpunched tickets were issued – as they had been on the trams ever since they began operation.

Church, who had not believed in tickets, went, as we have seen, in early 1891. That same year, on May 31, the L.G.O.C. introduced Road-Car-type tickets, putting up the wages of drivers and conductors at the same

The first L.G.O.C. Bell Punch tickets, of 1893. The backs of the tickets were used for commercial advertising

ciently alive to the problem to take the positive step of offering a £1,000 award for a system which could be shown to be efficient. Ideas rolled in – 671 schemes were submitted – but none of them met the conditions. Trials showed that when tickets were used receipts dropped. The reasons are anyone's guess, but one excuse put forward was that a conductor had no time to issue tickets *and* keep a sharp look out for prospective passengers. One idea was that of J. N. Maskelyne, of the famous family of illusionists. His tickets had serial numbers, making it possible to trace who had issued them, and had a space in the centre in which the conductor was supposed to punch a number of holes corresponding with the number of pence paid in the fare. A printed legend on the ticket enjoined the public to make sure that the procedure was properly carried out – but the system lost money when tried out. Other ideas, familiar again today, included the

time in an attempt to compensate in some part for the loss of unofficial 'earnings'. The effect, however, was greater than had been expected, for while the L.G.O.C. did not issue tickets there seem to have been cases where Road-Car and tramway passengers did not get tickets and, with so much ticketless travel on the L.G.O.C. vehicles, did not notice the omission. Now, however, Londoners knew that they should get a ticket on practically all public transport in London and came quickly to expect to be given one.

After duty on the night of Saturday, June 6 – very late at night because they did not finish work until then – there was a meeting of bus crews and an immediate strike was called. The Road-Car and other omnibus company employees also joined in. The strike was officially for shorter hours, since it could hardly be for the loss of opportunity to help themselves to the takings, and the management agreed to a reduction to a

Building and repairing horse buses at the North Road, Islington, coach factory in 1904

12-hour day plus, in most cases, an increase in earnings. This strike is of interest in that it was one of the first in which a trade union was involved. Thomas Sutherst, a barrister, had formed a trade union in 1889 to represent mainly tramwaymen, though a few busmen had joined. Sutherst gave the men his advice during this dispute and, on their behalf, accepted the new conditions on June 13. (In fact, the 12-hour day did not last long and crews were soon back to a 15-hour day at a slightly increased wage). R. G. Hall, who had not impressed the shareholders in this affair, was asked to resign in 1893 after a shareholders' inquiry into the company's affairs. Refusing to resign, he found himself dismissed.

Other changes came about during this period. For example, the iron steps at the rear of most buses were metamorphosed into curving flights of steps leading from greatly enlarged platforms. This important change, together with the reduced fares on many routes, increased the popularity of buses and encouraged the use of both decks by both sexes. There also appeared a number of single-deck one-man-operated buses on short routes which charged a flat fare of one halfpenny. This had to be placed in a glass-sided box under the supervision of the driver, anticipating by many years the 'Johnson'-type box used on some flat-fare routes today. These short routes, such as the one between Smithfield Meat Market and Stamford Street, Blackfriars Road, acquired the name of 'halfpenny bumpers'.

One of the results of the strike was a period of peace between the L.G.O.C. and the Road-Car Company, with even, at one time, an attempt to use joint time-keeping officials. This seems to have foundered because the ordinary busmen were less willing

Traffic congestion in Fleet Street in 1897, with 'garden-seat' buses well patronised

Motive power in 1901—the stables at Mare Street, Hackney

to forgive and forget former rivalries than were the members of the respective boards, but at the higher levels co-operation continued with, in some areas, a joint fares policy. The two main companies were joined in fares agreements by Andrews' Star Omnibus Company, which had star-surmounted poles to distinguish its buses, and the London Omnibus-Carriage Company.

The period of truce continued to the end of the century, and in 1900 the L.G.O.C. had 16,790 horses working an average of 1,348 buses and covering 31,246,259 miles in the year. The year's passengers totalled 199,575,529.

Even now, horse buses carried no route numbers; the names of places served, painted in large letters on the sides of the buses, were considered to be sufficient identification. The L.G.O.C. was by then running over some 50 routes and working another 30 in conjunction with the ten horse bus associations of which

it was a member. Buses worked by these associations, though belonging to different owners, were often all of one colour for a particular route. This led to a profusion of bright colours on the London streets.

The associations in which the L.G.O.C. had a part were, in alphabetical order, the Atlas & Waterloo, the Barnsbury & King's Cross, the Camden Town, the Camden Town & Bayswater, the Farringdon Road, the John Bull, the Kingsland, the Victoria (or Victoria Station), the Victoria & King's Cross, and the Westminster. Apart from the association colours, the L.G.O.C. and the Road-Car Company adopted the same colours in some instances. Both, for example, ran white-painted buses on Liverpool Street–Fulham services and red ones on the Hammersmith–Liverpool Street routes.

As far as the L.G.O.C. was concerned, some attempt to clarify the routes of buses for prospective passengers was made by the

One of London's last horse buses, operated by Fred Newman across Waterloo Bridge, in 1914
—the last year of regular horse bus operation

addition of initial letters of routes at the front and rear of buses, though a stranger might have found it hard to guess that 'B.S. & V.' meant that the bus plied between Baker Street and Victoria. The company had in fact produced a numbering system for routes when tickets came in in 1891, but this was only to enable the staff to identify tickets. It produced another system using letters only a little later, but this again was for staff information.

The Indian summer of the horse bus continued into the beginning of the 20th century and in 1901 there were 3,736 licensed horse buses in London. The L.G.O.C. reached its own peak in 1905, with 1,418 buses and 17,000 horses. At that time the Road-Car Company had 520 buses. There were still some buses drawn, like the first of Shillibeer's, by three horses harnessed abreast. These were large, but old, 'Favorites' used on journeys to the

City in the early mornings, but every other bus had two horses except for a few four-in-hands which came in from the suburbs in the mornings, mostly carrying their regular passengers and charging higher fares for express services. They were, in their way, a throwback to the stage coach, though the vehicles were normal garden-seat buses. They lasted, surprisingly, until 16 March 1912, when the last one, owned by Thomas Tilling, made its final run on the Balham Hill–Gracechurch Street route.

A driver of such an express bus recalled in later life that he had 24 regulars on his special service from Swiss Cottage to London Bridge. He would collect them at their houses in the morning and each would take his own regular seat, the outside passengers wrapping themselves up in their own personal rugs. On May 1 the passengers would present the driver with a new whip, a grey

[38]

top hat, and a rug; and at Christmas he would have five sovereigns and a brace of pheasants.

The giving of gifts to busmen was not unusual, especially on the routes with 'regulars', but the best-known of such practices was Lord Rothschild's habit of giving a brace of pheasants to each busman every Christmas. At that season the drivers' whips all sported the Rothschild racing colours.

Incidentally, even the 'in-town' buses would sometimes begin their first trip of the day by collecting regular passengers from their own doorsteps.

The L.G.O.C. built its last horse buses in 1905 and two years later the last of the knife-board buses ceased to run. The first of the L.G.O.C. horse-bus routes to go went in early 1906 and the last went on 25 October 1911 – from the London Bridge–Moorgate Street route. These were not the last horse buses in London, for there were, at that time, still nearly 800 in regular service with other companies. From then on they dwindled rapidly until in 1914 there were only 63. The last of these, on Tilling's Honor Oak–Peckham Rye Station route, ceased operations on the evening of 4 August 1914 – the horses were wanted for war service. Thus ended the regular career of horse buses in London. They had fallen victims, after raising horse operation to an amazing peak of efficiency, to mechanization, a monster which had been haunting them since the Hancock steam buses had shown their paces in the 1830s almost at the birth of the bus era. How this change came about we shall see in the next chapter.

VI The Mechanical Age Begins

THE horse bus did not, of course, vanish from the scene with quite such rapidity as the end of the last chapter might suggest, but it was thought better to chronicle a clean ending before entering the mixed world in which horse and engine strove for mastery on the London streets – a struggle which was to continue, if not for bus work, very nearly up to the Second World War.

Not surprisingly, in view of the high state of efficiency reached by locomotive traction on the railways, the first experiments of the new era were with steam, but not to propel buses. It was the tramways, with their affinity to the railways, which first introduced steam locomotives to replace their horses. Successful as these machines were mechanically, and well as they ran on the Continent and in many provincial cities, the tramway locomotives were just too heavy for London tram tracks built with nothing more than horse cars in mind.

Although there were successful cable tramways at Highgate and Streatham, and the system was used in the U.S.A. to such an effect that the San Francisco cable cars are still a 'must' for every tourist, it was to electricity that the London tramways eventually turned. Already in use in the U.S.A. from the 1880s, the electric trams were clean and relatively trouble-free, and the choice of electric traction instead of cable for London's first full-scale deep tube railway, the City & South London, when it opened in 1890, was probably the final spur needed. (We exclude the short-lived cable-worked Tower Subway line which opened – and closed – in 1870. It was without doubt, although only 1,350ft. long, the world's first tube railway).

Apart from experimental workings, the first electrified London tramways were opened in 1901 by the London United Tramways Company – from Shepherd's Bush and Hammersmith to Acton and Kew Bridge.

The London County Council, which had had powers to operate tramways since 1896, obtained powers to work electric tramways in 1900. It had embarked in 1895 (under the provisions of the Tramways Act, 1870) on a programme of buying up most of the tramway networks in its area in order to bring some measure of co-ordination to the services, and by 1909 it had acquired 113 miles of tramway divided roughly equally between the north and south sides of the river. Its first electric tramway, however, did not run until 1903, by which time the municipal tramways of East Ham and Croydon had already been electrified. The L.C.C. route, when it came, was notable in that it did not use overhead wires. Its trams picked up power from a conductor hidden in a conduit beneath the road. All that could be seen on the surface was a narrow slot running between the tram rails. Through this slot passed the pick-up arm or 'plough', as it was usually known. A pattern developed in which this neat, but expensive, conduit system, with its avoidance of forests of posts and overhead wires, was used in the inner areas of London and the cheaper overhead system was used elsewhere. The 1903 line ran between Westminster and Tooting.

The tram flourished. One of its main protagonists, Clifton Robinson of the London United Tramways, claimed in a letter to *The Times* in 1905 (a year after the first electric covered-top trams appeared) and published in its Engineering Supplement, that there was a wide field of usefulness open to a really efficient type of motorbus – as a feeder to the tramways! Strangely, no tramways crossed the river until 1906. The buses, then, still had the cross-river traffic to themselves. The last horse tram was not withdrawn until 1915 – four years after the last L.G.O.C. horse bus and a year after the last of the Tilling horse buses. The trams looked secure in their comfort, cleanliness, and strength with the London County Council solidly behind them and bent on extending the system – by 1915 the L.C.C. had nearly 145 miles of electrified tramway.

The horse bus could not compete with the challenge from the new underground railways, let alone the trams. Despite the fact that more passengers than ever were being carried, the earnings of each horse bus fell lower and lower. Soon after the opening of the Central London Railway in 1900, giving easy and cheap access to both City and West End, the L.G.O.C. was paying dividends from its advertising profits rather than from carrying passengers.

The bus companies did not, of course, watch the march of mechanical progress without trying to do something about it. They were, however, hamstrung by the Locomotives Act of 1865 which laid down that mechanically-propelled vehicles should not exceed 2 m.p.h. in towns (and 4 m.p.h. in the country) and were to be preceded by a man on foot carrying a red flag. The 'Red Flag Act', as it was called (although the need for the man on foot actually to carry a flag was removed in 1878), remained in force until 1896. Its demise is still celebrated every November by the 'Old Crocks' run to Brighton – and it seems probable that it inhibited development of mechanically-propelled vehicles to a very great extent – after all, who would spend time and money developing an advanced road vehicle which he could never run in a town at more than 2 m.p.h.? It seems certain that efficient steam road vehicles could have been built in that age of steam if there had been any prospects for them. Another inhibiting factor – which the tramways escaped by having their own tracks but by the same token contributed to – was the shocking state of the road surfaces. Tramways, incidentally, had been allowed, subject to Board of Trade approval and licence, to use mechanical power from 1879 onwards.

The first mechanically-operated bus to have been licensed seems to have been a Radcliffe Ward battery-worked bus which ran trials in London in 1889. Little is known of this, except that it ran at a speed of about 8 m.p.h. (when the speed limit was still 2 m.p.h.!) and resembled 'a large and rather cumbrous omnibus', and it is often confused with a later 10-seater single-deck battery bus, also by Radcliffe Ward, which was owned by the London Electric Omnibus Co. Ltd. in which Radcliffe Ward was the leading figure. This had two motors and drew its power from a battery of 72 lead-acid cells – which weighed 15 cwt. It was licensed on 29 December 1897. There was a good deal of opposition to the introduction of this vehicle and the initial Press trip was declared to have been ruined by sabotage. The small bus is said to have resembled a tramcar in outline and to have had 18-in. wheels – far more like a tram than a horse bus. The Radcliffe Ward had a much more successful second public debut and ran a 4½-mile round trip at an average speed of 8 m.p.h. despite persistent attempts to block its way *en route*. It made many other demonstration trips and two similar buses were built, but none went into public service. The snag, as with battery-operated vehicles even today, was the weight of the battery and the need to keep it constantly charged.

There were demonstrations in London by a steam bus in 1897 and two by imported motor buses, both with Daimler engines, in 1898, but it was not until 1899 that the Motor Traction Co. Ltd. put London's first petrol-engined buses into public service. These had 12-h.p. Daimler-engined chassis with 26-seat horse-bus type bodies by Straker and ran between Kennington Gate and Victoria via Westminster Bridge from October 9. There were two of these buses, apparently working at some periods on alternate days, but even so the combination of bad road surfaces and their metal tyres seems to have been too much for them. They were constantly breaking down during the year or so that they lasted on that route and the Kennington Gate–Oxford Circus route to which they were transferred early in 1900.

In January of the same year (1899), steam had made its expected re-appearance in the shape of a steel-tyred double-deck 24-seater by E. Gillett & Company of Hounslow. This bus seated 10 on the lower deck and 14 on the upper, the upper deck passengers being shielded by a light canvas canopy from the smoke and smuts from the chimney. The bus, owned by the Motor Omnibus Syndicate Limited, was duly licensed on 21 January 1899 by the Metropolitan Police and ran demonstration trips, but not in regular service. The L.G.O.C. had an offer from the Pennsylvania Steam Vehicle Company in August 1901 to build a motor vehicle which was claimed to be able to give a great reduction in working expenses, but the L.G.O.C. delayed consideration of the offer and nothing seems to have come of it.

The next foray of the L.G.O.C. into mechanical buses seems to have been the ordering, at a cost of £450, of a 30-passenger Fischer petrol-electric bus in June 1902, but when the chassis arrived from the U.S.A. the following April and was fitted with a double-deck body it could not obtain a licence, the police declaring that it was too wide to be classified as a 'light locomotive'. The bus eventually obtained special sanction for its use and ran trials but was offered back to its builders in October that year, the L.G.O.C. asking for its money back. The main reason for failure, apart from size, seems to have been the very high petrol consumption.

The story of these early experimental buses is by no means easy to trace. Although vehicles were licensed there was no system of registration until the Motor Car Act of 1903 required it from 1 January 1904, when the first 'number plate' appeared, and many remarkable attempts probably went almost unrecorded. No fewer than 13 double-deck and 79 single-deck mechanical buses were licensed in 1899–1904 (inclusive). One which was well authenticated, however, was the 1902 venture of the London Road-Car Company into steam buses with a Thornycroft chassis, similar to that of the coke-fired lorries supplied for the Boer War, on which was mounted a converted and enlarged 36-seat horse bus body with canopy and side curtains for the upper deck. The venture was a joint one between the bus company and the manu-

The short-lived Fischer petrol-electric bus ordered by the L.G.O.C. in 1902.
After a few months' trial in 1903 it was decided to return it to its builders

facturers, the builders supplying the chassis, fuel, lubricating oil, and the driver, and the Road-Car company the body, the equipment, and the conductor. The arrangement was that the bus company would pay Thornycroft's a shilling a mile and keep the rest of the receipts, but after some weeks on the Hammersmith–Oxford Circus route it was found that the bus was costing Thornycroft's 1s. 6d. a mile and taking only 11d. a mile, on average. Mechanically it seems to have been quite successful – though described at the time as 'the sensation and the distress of Bayswater Road and Oxford Street in the summer of 1902' (and by the vulgar as 'the twopenny lodging house') – but obviously the financial loss could not continue. There also seems to have been some argument about who

should pay the repair bills after a collision with a tramcar. In the end the builders took the bus back and sold it to an operator in South Africa, where it seems to have run quite happily for some years. The Accountant of the L.R.C.C. at the time, J. C. Mitchell, is reported as saying, 'This steam bus was the first business motor bus in my view, but it was a calamitous effort. . . . I have never heard of it since (it went to South Africa) and neither, do I think, has Sir John Thornycroft'.

East Ham was the scene of another steam experiment in 1903 with a service run for a few months by a Clarkson bus between North Woolwich and the Royal Albert Docks. The bus was hired from its Chelmsford builders who also supplied the L.G.O.C. with an oil-fired steam bus with which it ran its first mechanical service. The bus was a single-decker with 16 seats and ran from 10 October 1904 to 7 June 1905 between Hammersmith and Piccadilly Circus. The working loss over this period was £319 18s. 5d. and it was decided that it must be withdrawn. It had, however, convinced the L.G.O.C. that mechanical traction must come.

The economic lesson that a single-decker could not pay was taken to heart also by the L.R.C.C., which, after trials with two single-deck Clarkson steam buses at the same time as the L.G.O.C. experiment, on 5 September 1905 put a double-decker Clarkson steam bus into operation between Hammersmith and Oxford Circus. (The two single-deckers were withdrawn in the previous month.) This was followed by a similar bus run by the L.G.O.C. between Canning Town and Oxford Circus (later extended to Barnes) in 1906–1907. But all this was too late. The petrol bus was already taking over.

Nevertheless, there was another determined attempt to establish the steam bus with the incorporation of the National Steam Car Co. Ltd. on 19 June 1909. The company was formed to promote the Clarkson steam bus and to operate it in London. The first service, with four double-deck buses, began on 2 November 1909 between Westminster and Shepherd's Bush via Oxford Circus. On the previous Saturday a procession of gaily-bedecked vehicles had carried a party of boy scouts through London as an opening advertisement. In 1910 the service was extended to Peckham (Rye Lane) via Camberwell Green and at the end of the first year 17 buses were already licensed and 13 more were being built. In that year, 1,790,000 passengers had been carried and receipts were £11,000. The company's original garage was in Hercules Road near the present Lambeth North Station, but in 1911 a garage was built in Nunhead Lane, Peckham Rye, which eventually passed to the L.G.O.C. and in due course to London Transport.

By 1914 the National had an average of 184 buses licensed for its London services (it had

interests elsewhere) and was working its vehicles in conjunction with the L.G.O.C. on a guaranteed receipts basis, but maintenance became difficult during the war and the fleet had shrunk to 100 buses by 1917. Two years later the company withdrew from London. Its garages at Nunhead Lane and Putney were purchased by the L.G.O.C. and its routes were taken over by L.G.O.C. petrol buses. The last route to be taken over, on 19 November 1919, was the 12A between Shepherd's Bush and Dulwich ('Plough') via Oxford Circus. (Clarkson withdrew from the business in 1920 and with his departure the steam buses that the company ran in Chelmsford also went – and with them, effectively, the challenge of steam on the roads.) The company, renamed the National Omnibus & Transport Co. Ltd., continued to operate elsewhere in the country with petrol buses. The well-known names of Eastern National, Western National, and Southern National were those of its subsidiaries. It operated, by arrangement with the L.G.O.C., buses in the Watford, St. Albans, Berkhamsted, and Hemel Hempstead areas and, in the early 1930s, also to Hertford and elsewhere in the northern outskirts of London. The arrangement was ended in February 1932 and the 150 or so buses concerned were taken over by London General Country Services (which the following year became part of London Transport).

Brief mention must be made of the experimental services operated by various companies with small wagonettes – hardly big enough to be called buses but still operating bus-type services. Apart from a few 'one-man, one-bus' enterprises, the first real wagonette service was that of the South Western Motor Car Co. Ltd. between Streatham and Clapham Junction. This began on 1 April 1901, using two 10-seater Daimler wagonettes. The service lasted only for a few months, mainly because of the heavy running costs, but a new service between Putney and Piccadilly Circus was started by F. J. Bell on 18 September 1901. This used seven 10-h.p. Panhardengined wagonettes carrying six passengers inside and two alongside the driver. They had rubber-tyred wheels and rear-entrance open bodies. In bad weather a roof and fixed sides could be added, so that for their period they were probably comfortable vehicles. Somewhat larger single-deck Scott-Stirling petrol-engined buses with 12 seats were tried by the London Motor Omnibus Syndicate Limited on the Oxford Circus–Cricklewood route from 26 November 1902. This service ran for less than a year, but the company reorganized itself as the London Power Omnibus Co. Ltd. and tried again, this time with a Marble Arch–Kilburn service using seven buses: the service began on 18 February 1904. Other, slightly larger buses were added to bring the fleet up to 12, but the single-deckers were replaced by double-deckers in due course, the last being withdrawn in February 1906.

VII The Triumph of the Motor Bus

THE year 1905 began with an announcement by the London Road-Car Company, on January 2, that it intended to replace the whole of its horse-drawn fleet with petrol-engined buses – a brave statement at a time when there were only 20 motor buses working in London. That the Road-Car Company had its fingers on the pulse of progress was only too clearly shown by the subsequent march of events. By the end of the year there were 241 motor buses and by the end of 1906 there were 783. At mid-1908 the number had grown to 1,066 and at 31 October 1910 there were 1,142 motor buses and the mechanical bus had drawn level with the horse bus, of which there were also 1,142 at that date.

The rapid rise was due to the introduction of a really practicable bus – the Milnes-Daimler double-decker first used by Thomas Tilling's. The first of these entered service on 30 September 1904. The Tilling bus – one of three – was quickly followed by the first of two similar vehicles for Birch Brothers on 11 October 1904. These buses were true double-deck motor buses designed as such and not in any way adaptations of horse buses or uneasy combinations of lorry chassis and bus bodies. Milnes-Daimler had exhibited its bus at the Crystal Palace Motor Car Show in February 1904 and it created much interest. With its 24-h.p. engine and 34-seater body (16 in the lower saloon and 18 on the upper deck) it set a pattern which can be traced through bus development well into the 1920s and beyond.

In 1904 the L.G.O.C. set aside £20,000 for motor bus experiments. Early the next year Sir John Pound, the Chairman, declared that the company had studied the causes of the failure of all the pioneer services and had 'observed various difficulties gradually surmounted'. They felt, he said, that 'the time has now come when services of motor buses can be successfully run by us'. But he continued, 'I am not one of those who imagine that motor buses will bring in more profit than we have made in the past, but I believe they will form a solution of the problem of London's traffic'.

There was another important step forward in 1905. One of the highest costs to be considered in bus operation was that of the rubber tyres. It was not unknown for tyres to come off the rims at only 200 miles and steel tyres were the rule for heavy vehicles. However, in 1905 the tyre companies offered to supply solid rubber tyres at a contract price of 2d. a mile – very much less than previous costs – and at this price it became possible for all buses to have rubber tyres at last. (Not pneumatic tyres, of course.)

The London Motor Omnibus Co. Ltd., a

A London General Omnibus Company Milnes-Daimler bus of 1905

new company, entered the field with five Milnes-Daimlers on 27 March 1905. This company was the first to paint a large fleet name on the sides of its buses – in this case 'Vanguard', the idea of the company's traffic manager G. S. Dicks. Dicks also introduced service numbers, which appeared on the 'Vanguard' buses from 30 April 1906, and his board arranged with Milnes-Daimler that 'Vanguard' should have priority in the supply of its products. Thus, although the L.G.O.C. brought a Milnes-Daimler into service on 29 May 1905, it had to turn to De Dion for its own motor bus fleet. The De Dions were also 24-h.p. buses with 34 seats and soon became the most numerous in the L.G.O.C. fleet, although it also had a number of German Büssing buses supplied by Straker-Squire. The L.G.O.C. copied the Vanguard idea of a fleet name and from January 1906 began painting the fleet name 'General' in large letters on its bus sides. The

Road-Car Company also adopted the fleet name idea: in its case it was 'Union Jack'.

Even now the petrol-driven bus had not quite reached full acceptance and attempts were made to provide something better. Notable were the battery buses of the London Electrobus Company which ran between Victoria and Liverpool Street from 1907 to 1910. They failed, like other earlier battery vehicles, through the weight of their batteries, which made them slow and heavy – though many forgave them this for the sake of their silence, smoothness, and cleanliness. Something of the same smoothness was given by the petrol-electric drive adopted by Thomas Tilling's for many of its buses. In this type of drive the petrol engine drove a dynamo which in turn drove one or more electric motors which turned the road wheels. Though this drive sounds complicated it was in fact very effective and did away with the need for gears. It added to the weight and to the price of the vehicles but remained in extensive use with Tilling's in London and the provinces until 1930.

Despite the rapid change to mechanically-driven buses – or perhaps because of it – the first few years of the century were hard for the former horse-bus companies, which exhausted their funds on the conversion of their fleets, and also for the new motor-bus companies which often had insufficient capital. There was a good deal of bitterness between the old and new companies, including controversies about the supply of new buses to one or another of the factions concerned. In self-protection bus operators began to discuss amalgamations and on 1 July 1908 the 'General', 'Vanguard', and 'Union Jack' fleets were amalgamated into a greatly enlarged L.G.O.C. Between them the three companies then worked 885 of the 1,066 motor buses operating in London.

Police regulations for motor buses at this time were very stringent – not perhaps surprising when new types had been appearing one after the other and breakdowns blocked the streets every day. In the 12 months to the end of May 1906, motor buses were involved in 2,448 accidents and in 1906 a 'Vanguard' bus (on hire at the time) crashed on Handcross Hill with a loss of ten lives. The legal speed limit was 12 m.p.h., although in the hunt for passengers in the competitive spirit of the times this was often exceeded. The police were also vigilant in the matter of noise. After the two canopied steam buses already noted, they refused to allow any form of cover for top-deck passengers or windscreen for the driver. The unladen weight was restricted, in 1909, to 3½ tons.

The multiplicity of types led to the suggestion by Frank Searle, Chief Motor Engineer of the enlarged L.G.O.C., that the company should build its own buses to its own requirements, using for the purpose the overhaul works at Walthamstow which had been set up by Vanguard. The idea was adopted and the best features of all the buses which had passed through the hands of the engineers were put together in a single bus, known as the 'X' type. It weighed less than the stipulated 3½ tons but still carried the standard 34 passengers on longitudinal seats in the saloon and transverse seats on the upper deck. There was some trouble with the police over the noise level but it was licensed on 14 December 1909 and two days later it was in public service. It created a good deal of critical comment in that it incorporated so many features from other vehicles but in general it was a very successful bus and 61 of the type were built. The only real trouble was with the spur-driven gearbox, which was later replaced by a chain-driven type. In this form the 'X' type was the forerunner of one of the most famous buses of all time – the 'B' type.

The 'B' type, incorporating all the lessons learned from the earlier types, was built at Blackhorse Lane, Walthamstow by the L.G.O.C. itself. The initial order was for 60 buses and after these had proved themselves steps were taken to build the rest to fine limits hitherto unknown in motor bus (or many other vehicles) manufacture. The object was to have parts made to such fine tolerances that they could be interchanged between any buses, so that a part which failed could be replaced from stock at any garage. This principle was to remain in force for all future London buses until the 1960s. Almost the entire 'B' type chassis was built at Blackhorse Lane, production rising to 30 a week and even, at one time, to 60 a week. The design had been begun in March 1910 and the first bus was completed on 7 October 1910. It was on the road in public service 11 days later.

The 'B' type was London's first standardized bus. It cost only about £300 complete – a small figure for the time, probably because of the 'quantity production' methods used. It was also a very quiet bus with a degree of reliability new to London and probably, at that period, unknown anywhere else in the world. At the end of 1913 there were 2,500 'B' type buses in service and in that year they ran 55½ million miles. The mileage lost

*The first standard London bus—one of the 'B' type vehicles that ushered in
an age of reliable road transport for Londoners*

through mechanical troubles in the whole of that year amounted to only 0.02%. The London motor bus had arrived.

The mechanical efficiency of this bus was so high that it is worth quoting its features in some detail. The engine had four cylinders of 110mm. bore and 140mm. stroke (some later engines were bored to 115mm.). It developed 30 h.p. at 1,000 r.p.m. The three-bearing crankshaft was carried in an aluminium crankcase with white-metal lined phosphor bronze shells. The cylinders were cast in pairs with integral heads. Side valves were employed with exhaust on the offside and inlet on the nearside. The two camshafts and the magneto were driven by Coventry silent chains. There was no water pump, since thermo-syphon cooling was used with the fan driven, by means of a flat belt, from the crankshaft. The gearbox had three forward speeds and reverse and the clutch was a leather-faced cast aluminium cone in the flywheel controlled by a pedal and two laminated leaf springs. Steering was of the worm-and-nut type with a cast aluminium steering wheel. (It is interesting to note the amount of aluminium used even at this early date.) The radiator also used cast aluminium top and bottom tanks though the tube stack was made up of vertical plain copper tubes.

The frame was of the straight flitch-plated wooden type (i.e. a steel and wood sandwich construction) with front dumb irons bolted on, and the front axle was an Elliott-type beam with stub axles. The rear axle was worm driven and fully-floating. All wheels were cast steel on phosphor-bronze floating bushes and were shod with solid rubber tyres. The suspension consisted of laminated semi-elliptic springs all round, reinforced at the rear by flat-section volute springs. The internal expanding brakes operated on the rear wheels, with four fabric-lined brake shoes a wheel – two for the foot brake, two for the handbrake on independent exposed drums.

Bodies for the 'B' type were not built at Walthamstow. Many of them were built at L.G.O.C. works at North Road, Holloway, or at the other coach works at Olaf Street and Seagrave Road, and others by Hurst Nelson & Co. of Motherwell in Scotland, E. & H. Hora, C. Dodson, and other builders. The Hurst Nelson bodies were brought down to London by train and mounted on to their respective chassis at North Road. The Scottish supply was essential because the Walthamstow works were producing chassis at a much faster rate than the L.G.O.C. alone could produce bodies. As with the 'X' type, the 'B' type had sixteen seats arranged longitudinally in the lower saloon, and eighteen transverse seats on the upper deck.

The design of the 'B' type was largely due to Frank Searle himself with the able backing of Walter James Iden, who, after a few months as Searle's assistant, became Works Manager in December 1909. The success of the 'B' type was such that the last of the L.G.O.C. horse buses ran on the night of 25 October 1911 between London Bridge and Moorgate. This was only just over a year after the first 'B' type ran in public service on 18 October 1910. The December 1910 list of L.G.O.C. routes (with a drawing of a 'X' type on the front and the legend 'Open Air to Everywhere') showed 30 horse bus routes numbered (with gaps) from 32 to 92, and 21 motor bus routes numbered from 1 to 25 with Nos. 13, 18, 21, and 23 missing. There were also six Sunday routes, Nos. 1, 4, 10, 12, 17, and 22. These varied somewhat from the weekday routes of the same numbers. As yet, the L.G.O.C. did not issue a bus map.

The 'B' type carried a new standard form of route number on an oval board mounted on the canopy above the driver. At first, the word 'Service' also preceded the number itself and this wording was carried on when the

first illuminated route numbers appeared in April 1912. The destination boards were also standardized with the final destination in large capitals at the top of the display and the intermediate points in slightly smaller type arranged below. Although windscreens were not permitted by the police, the L.G.O.C. introduced shielding glass screens on both sides of the driver in April 1912. For some reason these were considered a safety hazard and some 18 months later they were removed again. Another safety device was the lifeguards fitted below the chassis in front of the rear wheels on both sides to prevent anyone being run over by being caught between the wheels. These lifeguards were fitted to some buses at the end of 1912, the bulk of the fleet being dealt with in 1913.

Service numbers had been used on the 'Vanguard' buses from 30 April 1906 and the Road-Car Company ('Union Jack') exhibited route letters from January 1908. Destination indicators at front and rear became a condition of police licensing from the end of August 1909, though many buses, including those of the L.G.O.C., already had them, and there had to be route boards showing the main points served on the way in geographical order in the direction of travel. These boards had to be illuminated at night. The old practice of putting route information on the sides was not forbidden, but if used it had to be in addition to the compulsory boards. Incidentally, although the interiors of buses had been illuminated since horse days – by oil, acetylene and finally electricity – it was not until 1916 that external side lights were made compulsory.

The first L.G.O.C. bus map, issued in 1911, showed 23 motor bus routes, but the one produced at the end of that year – the first 'all-motor' map – showed 44 daily routes with 12 on Sundays. The Sunday routes stretched out to such weekend resorts as Hampton Court.

The colour of the London bus scene faded with the multi-hues of the horse-bus routes, though apart from the red adopted by the

The first 'General' map, issued in March 1911, showing 23 motor bus routes

L.G.O.C. (which still exists on London buses today) there was the dark red of the Tilling buses. The white 'Vanguards' had gone into the L.G.O.C. but there were still the white 'National' steam buses. The 'General' buses carried uniformed conductors from December 1910, but the drivers received only caps and dustcoats for many years after that. The first L.G.O.C. school for conductors opened in a converted horse stable at Page Street, Westminster, in December 1912. A new, specially-built school was opened at Milman's Street, Chelsea, in the following year, and driver training, hitherto carried out at Battersea, was also transferred to Chelsea. This school remained in being until 1924 when the training was transferred to Chiswick – still the site of the training school today. Even in 1913,

the Chelsea school had a yard used as a 'skid track' and had its own cinema and slide projection room as well as other visual aids.

Training for the horse busmen was very much needed with the balance changing so rapidly in favour of the motor vehicle and the 'B' types coming on to the road at a rate of two dozen or more a week. A sign of the times was an item in the *Daily Mail* of 15 March 1912 (quoted in full in John Tilling's *Kings of the Highway*) recounting how 15 regular travellers met in the last of the four-horsed omnibuses to cross London Bridge to sign a petition to Tilling's that their regular driver 'Old Tom' should be allowed to continue to drive them up to the City from Clapham and Balham as he had done for 30 years. This solitary four-horse bus was due to be with-

[49]

drawn the next day – a Saturday – and 'Old Tom' himself was wondering whether he would be allowed to learn to drive a motor bus. But the bus *was* withdrawn, and Tom Rickman ('Old Tom') drove other vehicles for many years. He died on 20 January 1929, aged 76.

But wishes for the old times were being swept aside by hard economic facts. With the 'B' type the fortunes of the L.G.O.C. were rapidly turning and its shares were leaping in value. The change to prosperity, though mainly due to fine engineering, had its roots in the amalgamations which left a unit big enough to realize the economies of scale which precision engineering made possible. The first amalgamation of note was that of 1907 between the London Motor Omnibus Co. Ltd. ('Vanguard'), the London & District ('Arrow' – in which Frank Searle first entered the omnibus business), the Motor Bus Company ('Pilot'), and the London & Provincial. These four became the Vanguard Motorbus Company which, as we have already seen, was amalgamated with the 'General' and 'Road-Car' companies in the following year.

The tale was not all one of amalgamations – there were working agreements, too. For example, a fares agreement was reached between some of the bus companies and the underground railways at the end of 1907, but mainly the accommodations were between bus companies – as with the sharing arrangement made between Tilling's and the L.G.O.C. in 1909. This followed the break-up of the old Associations.

Early in 1911 the L.G.O.C. absorbed the Great Eastern London Motor Omnibus Company, and later in that year there were negotiations with the Underground company, which saw in the 'General' the ready means of running buses as feeders to its railways to the profit of both – and incidentally following the spirit of the findings of the Royal Commission on London Traffic, set up in 1903 to conduct an inquiry for the first time into London traffic. The Commission's report, published in 1905, was in favour of establish-

ing a London Traffic Board with general powers over the provision of public transport in London. The acquisition of the 'General' would allow a degree of co-ordination between rail and bus services. The L.G.O.C., realizing that other bus operators with equally-successful buses could come into the market at any time – there were no restrictions on entry into the business – saw the wisdom of joining forces with the railways, and financial control duly passed from 1 January 1912. The headquarters of the L.G.O.C., which since 1908 had been in the old Road-Car offices at 9 Grosvenor Road, moved to Electric Railway House – now part of London Transport's 55 Broadway headquarters but then the headquarters of the Underground.

With the takeover came moves to ensure closer interworking between the buses and the Underground. Many bus services were reorganized to begin and end their journeys at railway stations, especially in the suburbs, so that for the suburban passenger, in particular, there was a great improvement in services, especially as through bookings were introduced. Some of the 'country' routes served many years before by horse buses but long since dropped were revived in whole or in part. The first, in 1912, was a Hounslow–Windsor service, conceived as an extension of the District's railway services from its Hounslow terminus, but there were also daily journeys to St. Albans, Sidcup, and other comparatively distant points. These effective extensions to the bus/train network were to play a considerable part in the development of London, housing tending to concentrate on routes on which householders knew they could rely.

The 'General' made a working agreement with the Associated Omnibus Company on 2 October 1912; took over the routes of the Metropolitan Steam Omnibus Company on 16 October 1912; and on 1 January 1913 began to implement working arrangements agreed with the New Central Omnibus Company. Twenty-one days later another agreement came into operation – this time with the British Automobile Traction Company – and only six days after, on 28 January 1913, the first of the new dark blue buses of the Tramways (M.E.T.) Omnibus Company entered service, worked under agreement by the L.G.O.C. Behind the establishment of this company had been the fear of the Metropolitan Electric Tramways that, after amalgamation with the Underground the 'General', previously limited in the area in which it could operate, would be allowed to expand into a much wider area. This in fact happened, with the 'General's' radius of action extended from 15 miles to within 30 miles of Charing Cross.

Shortly after the M.E.T. had placed orders for a large fleet of Daimler buses, however, the British Electric Traction Co. Ltd. (of which the M.E.T. was a subsidiary) concluded a comprehensive agreement with the L.G.O.C. in November 1912 defining the area outside which the L.G.O.C. agreed not to operate, and making working arrangements for all traction business within the London area. As a result, the London & Suburban Traction Co. Ltd. was incorporated on 20 November 1912 as a joint enterprise of the Underground Group and the B.E.T. Group. It immediately took over control of the M.E.T. (from the B.E.T.) and the London United Tramways (which the Underground had owned since September 1902), and in May 1913 another B.E.T. company – the South Metropolitan Electric Tramways – was added.

The 300 or so buses the M.E.T. had ordered to run through its subsidiary bus company in self-defence against the 'General', therefore, went straight into the larger company's fleet between January and August 1913. These buses were Daimlers and noted for the quiet running of their sleeve-valve engines.

Good as it was, the 'General' did not rest on its laurels with the 'B' type but sought to improve it – no easy matter within the weight and speed restrictions of the day. One ingenious idea was a 'bentwood' body with curved side panels below the waist line. This construction gave enough extra space to mount the inside seats *across* the body instead of longitudinally. There was not enough space, even then, for the modern style of seating and the engineers had to mount a double seat on one side of the gangway and a single seat on the other. Steel bodies were also tried and on the drawing board was a bus with a side entrance instead of the rear platform and another designed for 'pay-as-you-enter' working. A single-deck version was built and operated – the first being used on 21 November 1912 for a service through the Blackwall tunnel. These single-deck 'B' types seated 16 passengers.

And so the tale continued – on 5 April 1913 the routes of the Gearless Motor Omnibus Company (which had become an associate of the London & Suburban Traction) were begun by the L.G.O.C. under agreement; on August 1 the South Metropolitan Tramways introduced buses under the fleet name 'Southern' by a similar agreement. In December a working agreement was made with the National Steam Car Company; on 2 April 1914 a working arrangement with Thomas Tilling; on 14 July 1914 the acquisition of the Metropolitan Steam Omnibus Company (worked since 1912, as mentioned above) and the New Central Omnibus Company (owned by the Underground from October 1913) – the latter's routes including some as far afield as Bedford. But on 4 August 1914 Great Britain was at war.

VIII The First World War

THE building of 'B' type buses went on at Walthamstow until June 1913, by which time 2,650 had been constructed. A few of these were sold to other operators – notably five to the United Automobile Company – and chassis were subsequently supplied for use as lorries by various firms. More than 160 of these chassis were, however, sold for use as lorries by the War Department, which, with gathering clouds on the horizon, was doing its best to advance from the horse age. Another 250 or more chassis went to the War Department to be bodied and equipped as ambulances. The supply of buses to the L.G.O.C. resumed in 1914 but it was not long before many of the buses were on war service. Even before war was declared 30 new single-deckers, each seating 20 passengers, were withdrawn on 1 August 1914. It is reported that by the same night their seats had been removed, ambulance fittings had taken their place and the buses were on their way to Dover.

The first venture of buses as such into war came when the French Government asked on 16 September 1914 for a contingent of British troops to be sent to France to give the Germans the impression that a full-scale British landing was on the way. This particular venture was organized by the Royal Marines and a staff officer, Colonel Ollivant, suggested that the effectiveness of the troops would be greatly increased if they had motorized transport and put forward London buses as the ideal vehicles. An appeal by the Admiralty to the L.G.O.C. for volunteers to act as crews was overwhelmingly answered and 70 buses, still in the 'M.E.T.' or 'Gearless' liveries, were shipped to Dunkirk. The crews were formed, with no further training, and still in some cases in their busmen's uniforms, into Royal Marine units. The buses acted as patrol vehicles, still wearing their London advertisements, in the Ypres, Lille, Tournai, and Douai areas, but this state of affairs did not last for long. The siege of Antwerp by the Germans took on a sterner aspect and the plight of those inside became desperate. The British government sent out another Naval Brigade to assist and the London buses (still in theory 'on loan' from the L.G.O.C.) were called on to take the troops from Dunkirk to Antwerp. The work performed by the buses during the short time they were at Antwerp seems to have opened the eyes of many military planners to their potentialities. They took food and ammunition to the embattled troops and took the wounded back to safety. When Antwerp fell, they carried not only wounded but many straggling soldiers safely out of range of the following enemy as the allied armies retreated towards the west, but the vehicles themselves suffered casualties and a string of damaged buses was left along the line of withdrawal.

Another call, this time for 300 buses and crews, was made by the Army in October. The men were enlisted into what was then the Army Service Corps and two companies – Nos. 90 and 91 – with 75 'B'-type buses each, were on their way to Avonmouth the day after enlistment. The buses were again still in their London liveries and with full advertisements. At Avonmouth the buses were loaded on to the *Eddystone* and ferried across the Channel and up the Seine to Rouen. There they were offloaded and driven to St. Omer. One of the drivers has reported that the first job they were given was to drive troops up and down from one section of the front to another to deceive the enemy into thinking the British Army was a great deal larger than it really was. While not an unknown military manoeuvre, this must have been the first time it had been carried out by a mechanized-transport force.

As soon as opportunity allowed, the buses were painted over with camouflage paint and

'B' type bus lost in action at St. Eloi in 1914—two weeks after leaving its London route

the windows on the lower deck were boarded up – reputedly less to avoid injury to their passengers from flying glass splinters than because the troops were always breaking them with their packs. The buses were prominent in the Ypres battles and the best known of them all – 'Ole Bill', now preserved in the Imperial War Museum – bears the battle honours '1914 Antwerp – 1915 Ypres – 1916 Ancre – 1917 Somme – 1918 Amiens'. 'Ole Bill' carries another plate reading simply 'London Scottish Ypres 1914' as a reminder that it was one of the buses which carried the first territorial battalion to see action in France into the first battle of Ypres – a battle in which in a single day 321 of the 750 London Scottish were reported killed.

It is difficult to assess the numbers of buses that actually went to France because several hundred of those requisitioned were used for various home defence duties. Also, many 'B' types carried lorry or ambulance bodies and many of those which did have bus bodies were converted to lorries or other types of vehicle during the war – at least two finished up as carrier pigeon lofts (mobile). It is generally accepted, however, that about 1,300 went overseas and some 300 remained in this country for defence work.

The manufacturing side of the L.G.O.C.

undertaking at Walthamstow was hived off in 1912 to a subsidiary, the Associated Equipment Company, and it was this company which built the war-time fleet. Prominent among the AEC engineers was George Shave, who was to become the chief engineer of the L.G.O.C. and, for a time, its operating manager. AEC later, needing more room, built a new factory at Southall on a 63-acre site and moved there in 1926-27. In 1933 AEC became an independent company, though still closely associated with London's buses, and it is now part of the British Leyland group.

One of the reasons for forming the AEC subsidiary was the possibility of sales of buses or chassis to outside interests, but the resources at Walthamstow were kept so busy with the L.G.O.C.'s own requirements that it was not until February 1913 that the first chassis was sold elsewhere. A working arrangement made between AEC and Daimlers provided that chassis should be built at Walthamstow and equipped with Daimler engines, and for nearly three years, from late 1913, chassis sold from Walthamstow, whether with Daimler or AEC engines, all bore the name 'Daimler'. This seems to have been in part because the AEC company was well known to be an L.G.O.C. subsidiary and an operator purchasing a new vehicle might not want his new buses to be too obviously connected with the L.G.O.C. – which might well be his commercial rival. The arrangement, in any case, seems to have worked quite well – possibly because Frank Searle, one of the designers of the 'B' type, also had a hand in the Daimler 'Silent Knight' sleeve-valve engine.

Before the war, the L.G.O.C., as we have seen, had been making great strides with its new buses and worrying the municipally-owned London County Council system with its large and – for the day – luxurious cars. Trams also had a comfort advantage consistently denied to the buses: they had covered upper decks. Now, with so many buses requisitioned and so many men volunteering for service in the forces, the tide turned. Trams used, indirectly, home-produced fuel and they could not be whisked away at a moment's notice to run in French or Belgian cities. By mid-1915 the London bus fleet was down to well under 2,000.

In these circumstances the L.G.O.C. put back on the road many of the 'X' type buses which had been withdrawn but not, fortunately, all scrapped. A number of lorries and vans also had bus bodies fitted to their chassis to increase the fleet. A temporary lull in War Department requirements beginning in autumn 1915 was used to obtain more chassis from the Walthamstow works and it was also possible to buy 100 or so buses and lorries back from the Army for use again as London buses. Some new buses were also obtained in 1916 although AEC, which had expanded enormously during the war (it supplied the War Department with 10,000 chassis for one type of lorry alone), was so heavily engaged on war work that civilian needs had to fall well down the scale.

Running the buses in wartime had its own problems. There was a blackout and buses had to run with minimal lighting at night. The reduced numbers of vehicles meant more crowded conditions inside them, for although so many men were away at the war the women were stepping into the breach. From June 1915 five standing passengers were allowed in the lower saloons of buses for the first time. Women appeared on the buses, beginning with Tilling's who employed women conductors from 1 November 1915. The first, in their grey uniforms with elastic-sided boots and hard, flat peak caps, worked on route 37. Next followed women conductors on the trams and on 14 March 1916 came the L.G.O.C.'s first women conductors.

Air raids began on 25 August 1916 with attacks by Zeppelin airships and more serious attacks by waves of Gotha bombers began in June 1917. By then petrol was getting short and some buses had to be cut, but even before that the L.G.O.C. had experimented with coal gas, alcohol-benzol mixtures, and other alternative fuels. A 'B' type bus with a coal-gas balloon where the top deck should have been, ran on trial along the Hammersmith Road, but the balloon blew about so wildly as the gas was used up and it lost rigidity that the bus had to be withdrawn. Another idea was also to run on coal-gas (which seems to have been reasonably satisfactory as a fuel) but to store the gas under pressure in more controllable steel cylinders placed below the lower-deck seats. Improvements in the war situation, however, came in time to cancel most of the work of installation, so that of the 20 or so buses earmarked for this experiment, on Route 16, only three went into service.

The end of the war by the Armistice signed on 11 November 1918 found London's buses depleted in numbers and sadly in need of maintenance. Of the 10,036 members of the L.G.O.C. staff who served with the forces, 812 died in action. As the survivors began to return to London, so did the hard-worked, much-battered buses. Among them was 'Ole Bill' which was chosen to carry a representative party of L.G.O.C. veterans to Buckingham Palace on 14 February 1920 when men and bus were inspected by King George V. The King showed great interest in the bus and its working and told the party that this was the first time he had ever boarded one.

[54]

IX Post War Problems and Progress

THE first post-war task was to build up the depleted bus fleet. The first additions were made up from the chassis of 30 or so 'B' type lorries and some spare double-deck bodies. These were followed by 250 new 'B' type buses, the chassis of which were built up by AEC mainly from spare parts left over from its war work. The bodies for these were found from stocks which had been in course of assembly at the beginning of the war and were now completed. These new buses were brought into service between late 1918 and April 1919. The War Department sold back over 150 'B' type buses and chassis which the L.G.O.C. considered to be in reasonable condition. Most of these were in service by mid-1919 and a relaxation of standards – on a temporary basis – by the police allowed another 250 buses in less good condition to be taken back from the War Department for further use. These extra buses received little in the way of attention, except for seats and new windows, and most of them ran in green or khaki paint with the name 'General' painted in white along the sides. They were known as 'Traffic Emergency Buses' and were put in service from June 1919.

There were also a hundred or so 'Traffic Emergency Buses' painted red. These began running from the last few weeks of 1919 and were made up of sub-standard chassis with standard bodies from various types of bus, including Straker-Squires and Daimlers. All these buses had the words 'Traffic Emergency Bus' painted in small letters above the rear wheels. The withdrawal of the Clarkson steam bus fleet in 1919 freed 60–70 bodies which were obtained by the L.G.O.C. and mounted on 'B' type chassis.

One of the 'red emergencies' was 'Ole Bill', but the care lavished on him must have improved his condition, for he went back into service for some years after the Buckingham Palace episode before final withdrawal. All the rest of the 'emergencies' had been withdrawn by the end of January 1921.

Another temporary, much photographed, expedient was the use of 180 lorries, on loan to the L.G.O.C. from the War Department, as temporary buses. The lorry-type bodies, with a temporary five-step staircase at the rear, were mounted on AEC 'Y' type chassis. (The 'Y' type chassis, used for thousands of lorries during the war, was more powerful and more robust than the 'B' type, being designed for heavy work in all conditions.) The lorry-buses had plank seats for 27 passengers and were surmounted by an open frame to which a tarpaulin cover could be attached in bad weather. They lasted for about six months from 2 June 1919 until 13 January 1920, and were then returned to AEC, except for a handful which were fitted with char-a-banc bodies and used for private hire work, for which the more powerful engines made them eminently suitable.

But the L.G.O.C. designers had not been idle during the war. Wonderful bus as the 'B' type had been, they already had something better on the drawing board. The 'something better' was the 'K' type. The first of these went into service on 26 August 1919 – a remarkable feat considering the difficulties of the time. The second 'K' type followed a month or so later and from then on there was a steady stream of them – 1,132 were built in all. The 'K' type broke away completely from the horse bus in having a lower body with arches for the rear wheels instead of being perched high above them. This enabled the body to be wider and thus to have, for the first time, the now familiar double cross seats on the lower deck. The driver was placed at the side of the engine, instead of behind it, so that the lower saloon could be extended forward. By these means the 'K' type was made to accommodate 46 seated passengers. Some

One of the 'lorry-buses' used for a time after the 1914–18 war to supplement the diminished bus fleet. This one ran a limited-stop service between Victoria and Liverpool Street stations

single-deckers seating 20–24 were also built, the first going into service on 12 August 1925 at Slough. They were the first L.G.O.C. buses on pneumatic tyres.

The engine of the 'K' type, like that of the 'B' type, was a 30-h.p. four-cylinder model, but incorporated the results of the progress in design that had taken place since 1910. It had an L-shaped head with aluminium alloy pistons instead of the former cast-iron and the maximum engine speed was increased to 1,500 r.p.m. Its compression ratio, however, was a little lower than that of the 'B' type engine – 3.94 : 1 against the earlier 4.13 : 1.

The same basic design was used in the 'S'-type bus, a 54-seater vehicle introduced in 1920, but the engine was of larger size, developing 35 h.p. at 1,000 r.p.m. and the compression ratio was raised to 4.15 : 1.

The first of this series – really a longer, heavier and more powerful version of the 'K' type – appeared in service on 21 Decem-

ber 1920, and all in all, including a few single-deckers from 1922, 928 were built. This bus weighed more than the maximum permitted 7 tons in force at the time, but it performed so safely and well that there was an official change of heart and the regulations were amended to permit a maximum weight of $8\frac{1}{2}$ tons.

In 1921 there came about a very significant change in the methods of overhauling L.G.O.C. buses. Before August of that year the annual chassis overhauls were carried out at the company's garages, of which there were 29 scattered throughout greater London. Body work and repainting was carried out at three 'coach factories', so that when a bus was due for overhaul it first went to a coach factory, where the body was lifted off for separate treatment, and then ran, as a chassis only, back to the garage for overhaul. After the mechanical work was completed, the chassis had to return to the coach factory to

*One of the 'K' type buses which broke away at last from the horse bus tradition by having a
low body with arches for the rear wheels.
The first 'K' bus appeared in 1919*

The first of the 'S' type buses, December 1920

be re-united with its body. This entailed a great deal of 'dead' mileage for the chassis and also meant that each garage had to be stocked with material for all its buses – which by 1921 could include 'B', 'K', and 'S' types, with others being designed. This led the L G O.C., mainly through the influence of G. J. Shave, to build a centralized overhaul works on a site at Chiswick. It was another step towards the efficiency which was already being attributed to the L.G.O.C. The mechanical standard already reached in 1921 can be judged from the fact that only three miles in 10,000 were lost because of break-downs. Chiswick was to reduce the overhaul time for the 3,000 or so vehicles from the 16 days needed at the garages to less than half that time at Chiswick.

George James Shave

A booklet describing Chiswick Works was issued by the L.G.O.C. in 1922 and it is worth examining to see how many later ideas were foreshadowed in this 31-acre plant with its 13 acres of covered shops – the main build-ing covered some 300,000 sq. ft. Building work actually began in September 1920 and by March 1921 some work was already being carried out in the coach-building section. The engineering side opened in August 1921 and by the following month 50 vehicles a week were being overhauled, the number rising to 75 a week by October. The standard designed rate was 100 vehicles a week, but there was an overload capacity enabling the number to rise, for short periods, to 120 a week. The labour force of 2,000 was almost equally divided between engineering and coach-building – and 1,000 of them could be served with meals in 15 minutes in the huge new canteen.

In the new works the 'flow' system was worked out to a nicety. The buses arrived at Chiswick under their own power, turned into the gates and ran to the west side of the works and, following direction signs, to the body demounting shop. Here the bolts hold-ing the body to the chassis were removed and the body was lifted by multiple hydraulic jacks clear of the chassis. The chassis was

driven off as soon as the body was clear and driven round the works to another gate on the opposite side to begin its own overhaul.

To follow the body first. An electric trolley was placed under the lifted body, which was lowered on to it. The trolley then carried it into the body shop, which had space for 104 bodies at any one time. On one side of the shop were stores, running the whole length, stocking any part which might be needed for the overhaul. The body was completely stripped and all the main components were reconditioned. This completed, the body was moved into the paint shop, which had space for 57 bodies. At this period the whole of the painting was done by hand, largely because four colours were involved and no successful method of masking the parts not to be sprayed with a particular colour was yet available.

For flat painting and first coats, palette knives were used instead of brushes with great success. The whole process of painting, with all its coats and final varnishing, took only five days and the results were said to be as good as those seen in the average expensive private motorcar of the period.

Once the painting was complete, the body moved into the mounting and finishing shop.

Traffic congestion is not new to London. This scene at Aldgate Tram Terminus in 1914 shows the confusion which a steam-wagon 'blowing off', a stationary tram, and some hand-carts could cause to 'B' type buses on Routes 78 and 23A

One day's output of overhauled buses from Chiswick Works during the 1920s

Chiswick Works from the air in 1966. The main works are in the background with offices in the foreground on the left. On the right of the main road is the training school for bus crews, with the canteen behind it. On its right, the well-known 'skid-patch' dotted with buses. London Transport's Research Laboratory is on the far right

Here it was fitted with cushions, aprons, boards, and advertisements, and electricians attended to the wiring and other fittings. The body was then ready to be mounted on a chassis again.

While the body had been passing through all these stages, the chassis, which had entered the other side of the works under its own power, was dealt with. As soon as the engine stopped the petrol tank was emptied and the fuel drained, via an underground pipe, into a main storage tank. The rest of the chassis was then dismantled, each part, as it was removed, being sent on its own particular route through the works by roller way or conveyor and completely dismantled. Every part was inspected and tested as it moved along its own route and worn parts were replaced by units from the stores.

Mechanical parts then, as now, got very dirty after a period on the road and special cleaning machines were installed at Chiswick to ensure that every part was clean and could

be properly inspected. In these machines, a tunnel big enough to accommodate items such as gearboxes was lined with a coiled pipe in which were thousands of $\frac{1}{8}$-in. holes. A hot caustic solution was forced through these holes under pressure so that every part passing through the tunnel was 'assailed by high-pressure jets from every angle.'

By the time the chassis had passed along the shop, engine, clutch, gearbox, brakes, both axles, springs, steering gear, and all other items had been removed until all that was left was the bare frame. The wheels went into a re-tyring shop with the tyre store immediately adjoining (still solid tyres, of course). The springs were heated in a gas furnace and retempered, after which they were subjected to a 50 per cent. overload test.

After the chassis frame itself had been inspected, repaired as necessary and passed as fit for another year's service, the process of reassembly began with all the items coming together from their own inspection and repair

A section of the general machine shop at Chiswick Works

The engine test house at Chiswick Works

lines at the right moment and in the right order to be reassembled with the chassis. The main reassembly moving platform was 220ft. long and it was possible to see an entire chassis reassembled on it in a few hours. Near the end of the platform the engine came into place for installation, having been through its own complicated and thorough dismantling, repairing, and rebuilding procedure. By the time the chassis reached the end of the platform it was complete again. There the radiator was filled, six gallons of petrol were put into the fuel tank (all oils, greases, and lubricants having been dealt with already in connection with the individual items) and a test driver climbed up into the seat. The chassis continued along the assembly path until it reached a position where the rear wheels were positioned over drums mounted at floor level. These drums rotated, the clutch was engaged so that the rotation of the rear wheels turned the engine and started it, and the tester drove the chassis away and out on to test roads built around the works, including a stretch of deliberately badly-surfaced road and 1 in 15 test hills. There were 800ft. of roadway with a double hill – enough sand and gravel was obtained from the excavations needed to supply the builders of the works with all they needed. On completion of the test run – successfully, of course – the chassis was handed over to the licensing department. Its task was to see that everything about the chassis was up to the current standard demanded by the Metropolitan Police.

Then, and not until then, the chassis retraced its path to the other end of the works and ran on to a carefully registered track over which its body was suspended, held by massive hydraulic jacks similar to those which removed it when the bus entered the works. The body was lowered on to the chassis – the jacks were so constructed that any minor misalignment due to the chassis not being in exactly the right place could be compensated for in the re-assembly. The bolts were passed through and tightened, the electrical leads connected, and the bus was driven off – not

yet back to the garage but to a Police 'passing station' where it could be officially inspected and passed fit for further service. In practice, the bus was almost like new again after this very thorough procedure.

Apart from these main activities, the works also had an experimental shop where new ideas could be tried out and a laboratory for testing fuels, lubricants, paints, and all kinds of materials used in the repair of London's buses.

Although there have been variations over the years, some of which will be mentioned in the course of this book, and the overhaul of bodies and chassis frames is now undertaken at Aldenham instead of Chiswick, leaving Chiswick to deal with the mechanical parts, the process described is very similar to that used today for the 'jig-built' buses, such as the 'RT' and 'RM' types, built to London Transport's own requirements.

The L.G.O.C. now had both the 'K' and 'S' type buses in service as well as, still, a large number of 'B' types – some of them of improved design – but a new bus, the 'NS', was on the stocks and promised to be a great improvement on any of those yet in service. Before the first of the 'NS' buses came on to the road, however, a new chapter of competition opened which was to have far-reaching consequences.

Although the L.G.O.C. and its associates had a virtual monopoly of London's bus traffic in 1922 it was largely because they had bought up, or come to an agreement with, any opposition. It was open to anyone who had a suitable vehicle and could get the police to license it to begin running bus services in the capital. This loophole did not remain untested for long. On 5 August 1922 Arthur George Partridge, with the backing of Christopher Dodson, introduced a handsome new Leyland bus, the 'Chocolate Express', on route 11. It was the first of the 'Independents' or, more popularly, 'pirates' which were to enliven, and later confuse to a point where Parliament had to take a hand, the London bus scene.

One of the smart double-deckers of the Chocolate Express Omnibus Co. Ltd.
They ushered in a new age of independents (or 'pirates') in the 1920s

The 'Chocolate Express' was hailed with delight by Press and public alike. No doubt after the rigours of the wartime bus scene this newcomer was a harbinger of things – better things – to come. The L.G.O.C., however, could see already that unregulated newcomers would play havoc with the provision of good services. The 'Express' found itself boxed in with an L.G.O.C. bus running immediately in front of it and another just behind.

The worst fears of the L.G.O.C. were realized. The 'Express' buses were well turned out and well managed, but after them came others. One of the next was the aptly named 'X-Service' Straker-Squire bus operated by L. S. Punnett. By the end of 1922 there were 10 independent buses in London. By the end of 1923 there were 194 and a year later nearly 500. The peak came at the end of

1925 with 197 owners operating 556 buses. The trickle had become a flood when ex-service men, looking for a new start in life, sank their capital into new buses which builders were only too pleased to sell on reasonable terms in order to have their paces shown on the London streets. This source was supplemented by further buses returned from the war, painted up smartly regardless of mechanical condition and sold to eager would-be bus owners – many of whom must soon have been sadder but wiser men.

The age of colour returned to the streets with these buses and imaginative names could be seen everywhere. Among them were 'A.1', 'Admiral', 'Birch' (back again after many years), 'British Lion', 'Cambrian', 'Carlton', 'City', 'Criterion', 'Drake', 'Eagle', 'Eclipse', 'Empire's Best', 'Felix', 'Field Marshal', 'Fleet', 'Havaride', 'Independent',

'Matchless', 'New Era', 'Nil Desperandum', 'Orange', 'Overground', 'Peraeque', 'Pickup' (very apposite but actually the name of the proprietor, Charles H. Pickup), 'Pioneer', 'Pro Bono Publico', 'Public', 'Red Rose', 'Redline', 'Renown', 'Supreme', 'Tally Ho!', 'The Rogue', 'Tottenham Hotspur', 'Uneedus', 'Victory', 'Westminster', and many others.

One very ingenious proprietor named his single bus 'Genial', but the return tickets he issued appeared so frequently on 'General' buses that the L.G.O.C. obtained an injunction against the use of the name and the 'Genial' became 'Buck'.

It may be thought that all this competition was a very useful spur to the established fleets and that the independent buses were a good thing for Londoners. In some cases, where the new owners conducted their fleets in an ethical manner and ran regular services, they probably were. There were, however, especially in the smaller fleet ranges of 1–5 buses, many unscrupulous owners who deservedly brought upon themselves the name of 'pirates'. They left the early morning, middle-of-the-day, and late evening services when buses were half-empty and most costly to run, to the L.G.O.C. and its associates. Then, in the peak hours, when the L.G.O.C. should have been earning, with full buses, the money to keep the less well-filled services going, the 'pirates' would swoop down upon the bus queues, fill up with passengers and be on their way. As soon as traffic on one route fell they would switch to another where more money was to be earned. It was not unknown for a pirate, espying a promising bus queue when he had only a few passengers on board, to give his passengers their money back, turn them off the bus, and race down to the new queue before a 'General' could appear in sight.

This state of affairs could not continue. Although the L.G.O.C. introduced its larger, more powerful 'NS' type bus on 10 May 1923, and put on more buses, it suffered severely at the hands of the 'pirates'. The company

eventually issued a plain warning that if the independents continued to 'cream off' its most lucrative traffic it would be compelled to cut out its unremunerative services. As *Modern Transport* pointed out at the time (in 1922), the 'great merit of the co-ordination and amalgamation policy of the big company has been that it has, by pooling paying and non-paying routes together, permitted of some routes being worked primarily in the public interest rather than with a view to immediate profits'.

The end of chaos – for the time being – came with the London Traffic Act of 1924, which permitted the Minister of Transport to designate certain streets as 'restricted streets'. The maximum number of buses allowed to run in such designated streets was laid down by the Minister. Every operator had to have his schedules approved and he might find that the route he was given to work differed in some respects from the one for which he had applied. Even more, the independent had to provide a proper service all day – not just dash out for a quick profit in the peak hours. The regulations relating to the condition of vehicles at the annual police inspection were more rigorously enforced and the maintenance level needed to achieve this standard was often too high and expensive for the very small operator. Some of them referred bitterly to the Act as the 'London General Salvation Act'.

This did not end the 'independents' story, but before we go on we must take a closer look at the 52-seater 'NS' type – another important milestone in the story of the London bus. The 'NS' is claimed by many to have stood for 'No Step', and this would have been appropriate since the 'NS' was the first L.G.O.C. bus with a dropped frame, lowering the centre of gravity and eliminating the step to the rear platform. The L.G.O.C., however, always claimed that 'NS' stood for *Nulli Secundus* and this, too, would have been very suitable since the bus was the first to be designed with a low centre of gravity in order that a covered top could be fitted to the upper

*An 'NS' type bus with solid tyres and open top compared with
the later transformation with pneumatic tyres and covered top*

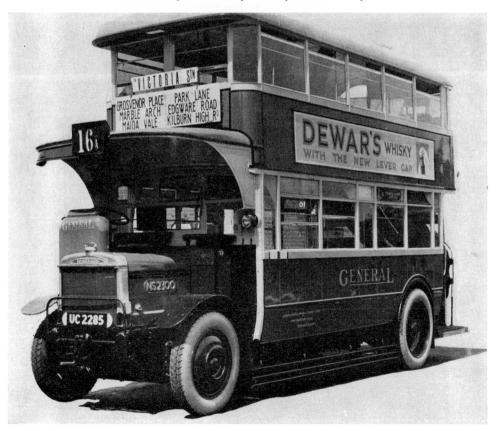

deck. The design was a little too advanced, however, for the authorities and the first of the 'NS' family had to enter service with open tops. It was another two years before the police would allow the covered tops to be fitted. As can be imagined, this new bus was the L.G.O.C.'s main answer to the 'independents', but it has to be confessed that some of the better vehicles they owned were at least as good as – and some thought better than – the 'NS'. The Leyland and Dennis buses, in particular, had their devotees. The 'NS', however, had a long life to come. The covered tops were fitted from 1925 after tests on the country routes had shown not only that they were perfectly safe but that the public liked them. Although not the first to have pneumatic tyres, they began to be fitted with them from 1928. Some of these buses were still running in London's service in 1937, the last of a class which numbered 2,378 in all. An 'NS' was the last solid-tyred bus to run in London – on 14 April 1937. They also had the distinction of providing from their number the first London buses with a totally enclosed staircase – fitted to a special version built in 1927 for the Blackwall Tunnel service.

To return to the 'independents'. It was not long before some found the pace too hot and retired from the business, sometimes selling their buses to other operators. Some of the bigger operators were ready to sell out to the L.G.O.C. but first, worried by the provisions of the 1924 Act and the schedules they had all had to deposit by December 1924, the 'independents' held a full-scale meeting at Westminster Central Hall in April 1925. The meeting was called by the Association of London Omnibus Proprietors, representing 195 concerns but not, of course, including the L.G.O.C. and its associates – a grand-scale 'Hamlet' without the prince. The meeting decided that its members, from May 14, would introduce new fares which would undercut the 'General' by 25 per cent. But when the time came the members could not agree among themselves what fares should be

charged and the whole thing seems to have petered out. Mention of the Association recalls that it would appear that it was its Secretary, in a *Morning Post* interview, who first 'officially' described his own members as 'pirates'. Whatever the L.G.O.C. may have thought of them, it appears to have been scrupulous in always referring to them, at least in public, as 'independents'.

As the 1924 Act was sufficiently daunting to keep most newcomers away from the business, the L.G.O.C. was able to reverse its policies of many years before and begin buying up the 'independents' without thereby encouraging others to start up in the expectation and intention of being bought up in due course at a profit to themselves. Even so, the policy seems at first to have been to wait for an approach rather than to go about making offers. The purchasing policy began to work with the acquisition of a controlling interest in one of the biggest 'independents' – 'Cambrian' – with its 52 buses in January 1926 at the 'Cambrian's' request. In March 1926 *The Times* reported that the L.G.O.C. was 'prepared to entertain any offers or proposals for clearing up the present situation', and a year later, with 200 of its rivals' buses already in its hands, the L.G.O.C. made an offer of £2,500 each for 'at least 350 of the 400 vehicles controlled by members of the Association of London Omnibus Proprietors'. (There were, at this time, another 77 independent buses running in London whose owners were not members of the Association.) The offer, which on any account must be reckoned a generous one as far as the average 'independent' was concerned, was met by an appeal from the Association to the Prime Minister to see 'fair play'. The appeal does not seem to have raised any satisfactory response from Downing Street.

Some of the 'independents', however, led by A. T. Bennett, managing director of the 42-bus 'Admiral' company, combined in July 1927 to form the London Public Omnibus Company. The new company absorbed 76 firms and 250 buses but on 11 December 1929 it was wound up, its buses passing into the L.G.O.C. fleet; the L.G.O.C. had obtained a controlling interest in March 1928. Other firms amalgamated or were absorbed but the independent omnibus operators did not pass finally from the scene until the formation of the London Passenger Transport Board effectively ended competition.

To turn for a moment to the 'General's' other rivals, the trams, it is notable that the advance of the internal-combustion engine and the flexibility it gave the buses had reduced the trams' two-thirds share of London's passenger traffic in 1911 to a half in 1921 and to about a third by 1927, even though the number of passengers being carried by the combined means of transport was steadily rising. The L.C.C. tramways showed their first deficit, after a quarter of a century,

in 1920. In 1924 the L.C.C. was considering substituting buses and 'the rail-less tram' (or trolleybus) for its conventional tracked trams. An attempt was made by the London United and Metropolitan Electric companies to revive traffic in 1931 with a very fine new tramcar – the 'Feltham' – and by the L.C.C. with a single new tram, known as the 'Blue Car' in 1932. In that year also the last piece of new tram track in London, in Westhorne Avenue, New Eltham, was laid. No new tracks were laid (except at the Vauxhall roundabout and diversions near County Hall for the Festival of Britain, 1951) and no new trams were built for London after that time. The age of the trolleybus had already been ushered in the previous year when the first trolleybus had begun running over 17 miles of former tram routes in the Kingston area.

X The New Bus Fleet

WHILE the battle with the 'independents' was in progress, the shape of the 'General's' own fleet was changing. The faithful 'B' type was at last coming to the end of its epoch-making career. The last double-deck 'B' was withdrawn on 9 August 1927, the last of the single-deckers lingering a few more weeks until 18 October. Meanwhile a remarkable new bus joined the fleet.

Designed from the outset to run on pneumatic tyres (or 'balloon' tyres, as they were often called), the 'LS' or 'London Six' ran on six wheels (three axles) and had a 50-h.p. side-valve six-cylinder engine. The double-deck body with its covered top and enclosed staircase seated 68. The chassis was built by the Associated Daimler Company, a name used between 1926 and 1929 by the Associated Equipment Company when it joined forces with Daimlers to produce the 'Associated Daimler' chassis. Twelve of the 'LS' type were built, with seating capacities varying from 66 to 72, some with enclosed staircases and some without, and one as a single-decker which, for a time, used petrol-electric transmission.

The Associated Daimler Company built an 'LS' to carry some of its staff to work at Southall and managed to pack in no less than 104 seats. It is no wonder that the 'LS' was popularly known as the 'Mammoth' – it was 30ft. long. The large size and the number of seats under cover would have made it a formidable opponent of the tram. Although not proceeded with, it probably provided many ideas towards the development of the later 'LT' type. The first bus began its career on route 16 on 4 June 1927; they were transferred for a time to route 29 and ended their days again on route 16. The last of the double-deckers was withdrawn on 16 March 1937. The single-decker's career spanned a much shorter period, from 22 July 1928 to 23 April 1935. Four of the double-deckers were converted to heavy breakdown tenders and continued to work as such until 1951. They were then sold to a firm of lorry-breakers which wanted them – not for breaking up but as towing vehicles.

Although not very successful in public service, the 'LS' type had shown the way to greater capacity and comfort with its long three-axle body and pneumatic tyres. Pneumatic tyres were not introduced with the 'LS' although, as already stated, it was the first bus designed to use them from the start. The pneumatic tyre came into service originally in 1925 on an 'independent' bus, but long before that the 'General' had been conducting trials with a 'K' type chassis weighted to represent a fully-loaded double-decker. The single-deck 'K' type buses got their pneumatic tyres within a few weeks of that first 'independent' – but it was to be another three years after the trials had been held before pneumatic tyres were authorized for the double-deckers of the class.

The 'General' was only too anxious to get its vehicles on to pneumatic tyres because buses fitted with them were allowed to travel at up to 20 m.p.h. instead of the 12 m.p.h. to which the solid-tyred buses were restricted. They also carried a 20 per cent. tax rebate. One difficulty was that buses fitted with them were not supposed to be more than 7ft. 2in. wide. The police eventually agreed that this could be increased to 7ft. 5in. on routes which were not shared with trams. As it was next to impossible to keep to 7ft. 5in. when converting existing buses to pneumatics because of the greater width of the new tyres, and so many of the L.G.O.C. routes followed the tram tracks, the 'General' found itself in a very difficult position. Fortunately deprivation of the comforts of pneumatic tyres on many of the busiest routes gave rise to a public outcry which eventually persuaded the police, in 1929, to give another inch and allow 7ft. 6in. wide buses to be operated in the Metropolitan Area – thus bringing London into line with the rest of the country. There had also been a change of heart on windscreens, enabling some of the 'NS' type and the 'LS' type to be fitted with them in 1928.

With the new regulations – and designed some time in advance of them in anticipation – a new breed of bus arrived, the first of which was the 'LT', which began running in public service on 6 August 1929. The 'LT' was a three-axle, six-wheel vehicle with an outside staircase (after the first 150 had been built an internal staircase was substituted) and seats for 54 or 60. Driver protection was provided following the change-of-heart on windscreens and in general the new bus took full advantage of the altered regulations. The engine used was made by AEC and had a compression ratio of 5 : 1 and a maximum useful running speed of 2,500 r.p.m. (At a later date the compression ratio was raised to 5.25 : 1.) It was a six-cylinder overhead-valve engine available in two sizes, one producing 37 h.p. and the other 45 h.p. This was the last and the most successful of the petrol engines used by London Transport; it provided the motive power of the 'LT', the 1929 'ST', and the first 250 of the 'STL' series which did not come into service until 1932. The 'LT' used an AEC 'Renown' chassis, which with two other closely related chassis – the 'Regent' and 'Regal' – made its debut in 1929.

The first 'LT' bus had seats for 54 – far fewer than the 'LS' – and this seems to have been a deliberate policy decision. The L.G.O.C. considered that the large-capacity vehicle had not shown up in the best light. Research undertaken into the optimum size of bus suggested that there must be at least 46 seats for a bus to earn a reasonable margin at the then current cost levels. On the other hand, if there were more than 54 seats (later, with a more modern ticket system, 56) the conductor could not get round in time to collect all the fares. This meant either that the bus was held up by the fare collection process and its speed along the route was unnecessarily slow or else that some of the fares were not collected at all.

Research of this type, difficult for a smaller

One of the L.G.O.C. 'LS' buses, or 'Mammoths' as they were known. As can be seen on the cowling, 'LS' stood for 'London Six', indicating the number of wheels

operator, was characteristic of the L.G.O.C. The tradition has carried on to London Transport days and is still a feature of London bus management. The L.G.O.C., however, found that the changes suggested as a result of its research were costly and difficult to introduce if they entailed important items such as, for example, a re-design of the buses. The scale of operations had grown to such a size that changes of this type were very costly and new items could take so long to introduce in the necessary quantity that, in the example given, the new buses could be out of date themselves before they had all been delivered. In practice, however, the London designs, despite – because of the scale of operations – their long testing periods, have generally proved to be so advanced that they have stood the test of time and remained modern and reliable when other vehicles

have appeared and gone. In this outstanding reliability the virtual rebuilding of the buses every few years at London Transport's own overhaul works has played a great part.

The first 'LT', therefore, conformed to the research formula and had 54 seats, 24 of which were 'inside' and the remaining 30 on the top deck. Trials with the first of the series seem to have brought about a change of opinion and the remainder of the first batch of 150 had 28 seats inside and 32 'outside'. Practice may not have accorded with theory, but the seating in later buses reverted to 56 and still later to 60 again. In all, 1,429 'LT' buses on AEC 'Renown' chassis were built, the last 10, and one experimental bus, having oil engines. Not all the 'LT' buses had two decks – 200 were 35-seater, single-deckers.

Almost simultaneously with the 'LT' there appeared a shorter, two-axle version, on an

[69]

A landmark in London bus history—the first of the 'LT' class of six-wheel buses. The remaining 'LT' buses had slight differences

AEC 'Regent' chassis, known as the 'ST' and seating 49 passengers, 29 of whom were on the top deck. Many of these buses were used by the 'General's' associates on country routes, but nearly 800 of the 1,139 built were used by the L.G.O.C., the first entering service on 1 March 1930.

Two more types of bus were soon to emerge. One was the 'T' type, used more by associates than the L.G.O.C. itself. The 'T' type was a single-decker on an AEC 'Regal' chassis and was seen as the ideal vehicle for the Green Line coach services which began in the 1930s. The earliest 'T' types had L.G.O.C. bodies and were fitted with six-cylinder over-head-valve petrol engines. These vehicles seated 30, but the later coaches had either Chiswick-built 27-seater bodies or 30-seat front-entrance bodies built at Addlestone by Weymann's.

The other type was the aptly-named 'Q', built and designed by AEC with L.G.O.C. interest. The conception of this unusual single-deck vehicle arose from an engine and transmission development allowing it to be fitted outside the off-side chassis frame member, tucked away under the body behind the front wheel. The resulting bus had a full front with passengers sitting where, apparently, the engine ought to be. The thought

*Early 'T' type bus, originally built for the L.G.O.C., in London Transport livery.
It is seen here as rebuilt with a forward entrance*

*Q1, with its engine behind the offside front wheel, was considered
a revolutionary vehicle when it appeared in 1932*

behind the design was that if the engine could be removed from its usual place there would be more room for passengers on a chassis of no greater length. The engine did, in fact, project above the chassis but this was disguised by fitting a longitudinal seat above it, much as similar seats on other buses cover the wheel arches. Because of the position of the transmission and final drive far out to one side, there was no room for double rear wheels within the permitted width, and single wheels were used. The 'Q' seated 37 passengers against the 30 or 32 more usual at the time. Q1 began working on route 11 on 5 September 1932 and excited a great deal of interest, mainly of the 'Where's the engine?' variety. It was at first garaged at Hammersmith but after its London debut was soon

Q 2—one of the two experimental front-entrance double-deck 'Q' type buses
—shown ready for running on Route 77

transferred to Nunhead to work in more rural surroundings. Development work on the design continued and a double-deck version was produced. Two of these were built and began running from Harrow Weald garage, on route 114, in 1934. The 'Q' was in production for only four years, but eventually numbered more than 230 vehicles of various types. It was used both in the red livery of the inner services and the green of the routes in London's country – we shall be coming back to the growing 'country' services later.

The main importance of the 'Q' type probably is that it was the first production bus to break away from the 'normal' position for the engine, preparing the ground for later under-floor engined buses and, in particular, coaches. It could even be said, by establishing the possibilities of an engine in a position remote from the driver, to be the ancestor of the rear-engined buses of today. The last 'Q' was withdrawn on 31 December 1954.

In 1932 also there appeared the 'STL', a long wheelbase version of the 'ST' seating 60 passengers, 26 on the lower deck and 34 on the upper which was extended forward over the driver's cab. The bodies were otherwise very like those of the later 'LT' and 'ST' types. Like the 'ST', the 'STL' was only a two-axle bus, so its seating capacity was remarkably high. It was also a very handsome bus despite its 'squared-off' appearance and, using the moquette-covered wood-framed seats with rubber cushions developed for the later 'LT' buses, gave a very comfortable ride. It was the last double-decker to be designed by the L.G.O.C. and was certainly a credit to the company. The first 100 of these buses arrived in 1933, with AEC chassis and Chiswick-built bodies.

[72]

A 'middle-range' example of an 'STL', the last type of bus designed by the L.G.O.C.

The production of the 'STL' was one of the final pre-war chapters in the struggle against weight which had been going on for years and was perhaps the key to bus design in the 1920s and 1930s. At that period a two-axle, four-wheel vehicle, fully laden with fuel, passengers, and crew, was not allowed to exceed a total weight of 10 tons. With six wheels, the weight could be increased to 12 tons – though some of the extra allowance was obviously taken up by the additional wheels and axle. Developments such as enclosed staircases, proper driver protection from the weather, and mechanical improvements such as more powerful engines, desirable though they were, all tended to raise the weight. With the six-wheeled 'LT' 60 seats were possible, but not with the 'ST'. The weight of 60 passengers, crew, petrol, water, etc. came to just over four tons, so that a four-wheel 60-seater bus would have had to weigh less than six tons empty.

The 'STL' chassis was designed to take a 26ft. long body – the maximum allowed at the time; but the big oil engine then beginning to make its mark with the fleet was too heavy and the well-tried six-cylinder petrol engine was adopted once more. By using light alloys where possible, and designing everything in the lightest possible way, together with the use of the light seats already mentioned, the L.G.O.C. produced its four-wheel 60-seater. After the first 100, it was decided to strengthen the structure and alter the body contour, reducing the seating capacity to 56. The reduction in seating capacity, by omitting a row of seats on the upper deck, made it possible to give the front of the upper deck a rearward slope and to round off the rear to give an even better appearance. Many versions of the 'STL' were built with varying numbers of seats for different purposes – no less than 2,679 were built, surpassing everything up to that time except the 'B' type – but none went back to the 60-seat layout.

Thomas Tilling also had some 'STL' buses, but they varied in detail and had only 56 seats from the start. One of these was the

Derby Day in the 1920s. Londoners flocked to see the Epsom Races and special fleets of buses were laid on to carry racegoers from Morden Station until well after the second World War. Here the advantages of open-top 'NS' type vehicles are obvious

first 'STL' to go into public service – on 29 October 1932 – the first operated by the L.G.O.C. began working on 3 January 1933. The last 'STL' was withdrawn on 1 June 1955.

A small but historically interesting class was the 'DL'. In 1929–30 the possibilities of metal-framed bodies were under discussion and the L.G.O.C. purchased one steel-framed body from Metro-Cammell. This was mounted on an 'ST' type chassis for trials and a few months later 25 more such bodies, each seating 20 on the lower deck and 29 on the upper, were ordered and mounted on Dennis Lance chassis – hence the 'DL'. They were not used by the L.G.O.C. itself but by one of its subsidiaries, Overground Limited, and worked mainly on the northern fringes of London. All were sold in 1937. A previous class of three buses on Daimler CH6 chassis,

the 'DST' class purchased in 1930 and fitted with ordinary 'ST' type bodies, was the first to introduce pre-selective gearboxes and fluid flywheels to L.G.O.C. practice.

Service tests with oil engines had begun in 1929 and in 1931 twenty-two of the double-deck 'LT' type buses were fitted with oil engines of the AEC-Acro type. A great deal of work was necessary on the oil engine to get smoke-free, smooth running coupled with reliability but eventually the AEC-Ricardo engine was adopted. In the course of time most of the 'LT' class were given oil engines. Because of the weight of the only oil engine to satisfy L.G.O.C. requirements then available – an 8.8-litre unit – the 'STL' class, as we have seen, was fitted with petrol engines. The later, lighter 7.7-litre oil engine changed the picture, however, and beginning with

[74]

STL 609 in 1934, all the later 'STL' buses were fitted with oil engines and also with fluid transmission.

At the end of 1933, six months after the formation of the London Passenger Transport Board, the total London Transport fleet consisted of 5,700 buses and coaches, of which only 180 had compression-ignition (oil – more commonly now called 'diesel') engines. By 1939 diesel-engined buses made up 65% of the fleet and had it not been for the war the whole of London Transport's fleet would have been diesel-engined by 1943. The war made this impossible, so the petrol engine lingered on for several more years, the last petrol-engined bus being withdrawn on 21 November 1950.

The special version of the 'NS' bus for the Blackwall Tunnel service has already been mentioned, and when the time came for their replacement it was done by 'STL' buses with bodies much modified at Chiswick to give more clearance to the roof at the sides of the tunnels and when passing other vehicles on bends. One modification of special interest was that to the staircase, which was arranged to turn a full 180° instead of the usual 90°: this change reduced the lower-saloon seating by one seat. Special tyres reinforced to withstand the rubbing against the kerb inevitably experienced in such narrow tunnels were fitted to the nearside wheels of the 39 buses concerned.

XI Unification: A New Era

THE idea of unifying all London's public transport under a single body was nothing startling – the L.G.O.C. had talked of it in its earliest years and so had many others – but it was not until the Underground group began to pull the various tube railways together and added trams and the L.G.O.C. to their empire that anything really effective was done. One of the believers in unified transport was Albert Henry Stanley, born in Derby in 1874 but taken by his parents, as a very young child, to the U.S.A. He made his name, while still quite young, as a manager of streetcar (tram) undertakings and by 1907 he was general manager of the Street Railway Department, Public Corporation of New Jersey.

He was invited to Great Britain to become general manager of the Underground group and took over that position on 1 April 1907. When Sir George Gibb retired at the end of 1910 Stanley became managing director of the Underground company. He was knighted in 1914, entered the Government in December 1916 and was made President of the Board of Trade. After the war he returned to the Underground Group, in 1919, as its chairman. He was created Baron Ashfield of Southwell in 1920.

Almost from the day when the 32-year-old Stanley arrived to take up office with the Underground he worked towards the co-ordination of London's passenger transport. Transport he considered, was a public service. It had to be adequate, efficient, and above all cheap, for, to use his own words, 'without cheap transport, a wide and healthy distribution of the immense populations of modern cities cannot be achieved and such cities made orderly, prosperous, and pleasant places to live in'. But cheap transport could not be provided economically under conditions of acute competition. Rate-cutting might benefit the passenger temporarily, but in the long run it could only lead to the bankruptcy of the undertakings involved. Lord Ashfield contended that the whole of the transport service must be paid for out of the proceeds of the part which was used. If the proportion not used (or, in other words, wasted) was by

Lord Ashfield—founder of London Transport

the L.G.O.C. to be pooled. The acquisition of some of the tramway interests in the London area and of bus services in the outer districts came next. The first legislation on the matter (apart from that connected with the setting up of the Common Fund in 1915) came with the London Traffic Act of 1924 which we have already noted.

Although born from necessity to curb the chaotic conditions of the time, that Act could be said to follow in the train of a long series of investigations by Government committees starting with the Lords Committee of 1863 and continuing through the Royal Commission of 1905, and similar bodies, some of which had recommended the establishment of a traffic board with far more drastic powers than those conferred by the 1924 Act.

No legislation could be simple to enact – there were too many interests to be consulted and considered – among them county, borough, urban district, and rural district councils, as well as local authorities and road and rail transport operators in the several counties concerned.

As far as the L.G.O.C. was concerned, the most important provision of the 1924 Act was that which produced lists of restricted streets (i.e. streets on which no additional buses were allowed to run) and the compulsory withdrawal of some buses where there was already overcrowding. The 1924 Act, however, was not enough in itself, and under the Act a London & Home Counties Traffic Advisory Committee was set up. In a report issued in 1927, this Committee urged the adoption of a common fund and common management for all passenger transport undertakings in the area, together with the establishment of some form of public control.

In the meantime, there had been advances on the railway front. In 1928 the four main line railways (L.M.S., L.N.E.R., S.R., and G.W.R.) agreed to associate themselves with the Underground Group, the Metropolitan Railway, and other urban transport undertakings in the pooling of traffic revenues in the London Traffic Area. The Underground

reason of competition increased, then, in a balanced economy, the only course of action left would be to increase fares. As he saw the problem, only by unified management and co-ordination could such waste be avoided, or at least considerably reduced, and his fixity of purpose over a quarter of a century was almost certainly the major influence in bringing unification about.

A select Committee of the House of Lords had reported on unification as long ago as 1863, but the first practical moves came, as we have noted, with the gradual development of the Underground group as a single administrative and financial unit with the formation of the Underground Electric Railways Company of London Limited on 9 April 1902, bringing together the District Railway, the Tubes and the L.U.T. This was followed, ten years later, by the acquisition of the London General Omnibus Company. In 1915 a statutory Common Fund was created which enabled the receipts of the Tube railways, the Metropolitan District Railway, and group, in partnership with the London County Council as owners of the largest tramway system, promoted two 'Co-ordination Bills' which provided for common management of their respective undertakings and the creation of an appropriate common fund. In Parliament the Opposition contended that these Bills did not go far enough or provide for sufficient public control. The 'Co-ordination Bills' failed to become law, though only by a narrow margin, because of an abrupt change in the Government in 1929. They played a major part, however, in preparing the ground for a much more ambitious bill introduced by Mr. Herbert Morrison in 1930. This bill, after some modifications to ensure Conservative support, was passed by the National Government and became the London Passenger Transport Act of 1933.

The new Board came into being on 1 July 1933 with Lord Ashfield as Chairman and Frank Pick as the only full-time member. There were also five part-time members, including Sir John W. Gilbert, a former Chairman of the London County Council. Frank Pick had been, like Lord Ashfield, one of Sir George Gibb's men. He had been Managing Director of the Underground companies and he now became Vice-Chairman and Chief Executive Officer of the L.P.T.B. His forte was administration and together Ashfield and Pick made a formidable team. But Pick was also a man of taste who left his mark on London Transport design in everything from typography and posters to architecture.

The duties of the new Board were defined in the Act and quoted in the Board's first annual report. It was charged with the general duty of providing an adequate and properly co-ordinated system of passenger transport for the London Passenger Transport Area and for that purpose, 'while avoiding the provision of unnecessary and wasteful competitive services', it was required to take from time to time such steps as it considered necessary 'to extend and improve the facilities for passenger transport in that area, in

Frank Pick

such manner as to provide most efficinetly and conveniently for the needs thereof'. The Act also imposed on the Board the particular duty to conduct its undertaking 'in such manner and to fix such fares and charges in accordance with the provisions of the Act as to secure that . . . revenues shall be sufficient to defray all charges required by the Act to be defrayed out of the revenues of the Board'.

The London Passenger Transport Area was defined in a schedule to the Act. More than three-quarters of its area was defined as the 'Special Area', within which 'no person or undertaking other than the Board may operate road services of stage or express carriages carrying passengers local to that area without the Board's written consent, except in certain minor cases. . . .' Within the Special Area the Board did not need a road service licence from the Metropolitan Traffic Commissioner, but public service vehicles on stage or express carriage services could be operated only on routes approved by him.

Within the 'outer' area, i.e. that part of the

L.P.T. Area not included in the Special Area, the Board could operate public service vehicles subject to the provisions of the Road Traffic Act, 1930, and to the grant of road service licences from the Traffic Commissioners. Outside the L.P.T. Area the Board could operate road services in special circumstances laid down, in accordance with working agreements with outside operators, or to the extent of not more than half a mile (one mile in Berkshire) in order to reach a convenient terminal point or stand. The Board could also work vehicles on private hire within the L.P.T. Area and outside that area within a radius of ten miles, or in the County of Kent five miles, from any point on the boundary of the Area.

Before 1 July 1933, the Commissioner of Police of the Metropolis was the responsible licensing authority for the Metropolitan Police District in respect of Metropolitan short-stage carriages, while outside that district this responsibility in respect of all public service vehicles was that of the appropriate Traffic Commissioner. The Act enlarged the area controlled by the Metropolitan Traffic Commissioner to include the whole of the L.P.T. Area and certain territory outside it. At the same time, the duties previously undertaken by the Commissioner of Police in connection with route approval, terminal points, and stopping places for short-stage carriage services were transferred to the Metropolitan Traffic Commissioner, who, however, was obliged to consult with the Commissioner of Police before giving his approval.

The Board's Special Area covered 1,550 square miles, and the London Passenger Transport Area 1,986 square miles. In addition to the Administrative County of London, the L.P.T. Area included the whole of Middlesex and parts of Bedfordshire, Buckinghamshire, Essex, Hertfordshire, Kent, Surrey, and Sussex. The population within the area was estimated at the time as over 9,400,000.

Before the establishment of the Board, passenger transport in what was now the Board's Special Area was provided by five railway companies, apart from the main line railways; 14 municipally-owned tramway undertakings; three company-owned tramway undertakings, and 61 companies, firms or individuals operating bus services under the provisions of the London Traffic Act, 1924. The majority of these were under separate management. All these undertakings were transferred to and vested in the Board by 31 October 1935, the date of the first annual report covering the year ended 30 June 1934.

Road transport undertakings already regarded as part of the Underground Group and therefore taken over immediately, apart from the L.G.O.C. itself, included London General Country Services Limited, Overground Limited, Morden Station Garage Limited (already belonging to the L.G.O.C.), Acme Pullman Services Limited, Bucks Expresses (Watford) Limited, Green Line Coaches Limited, and Skylark Motor Coach Co. Ltd. Also taken over were the London omnibus undertakings of Thomas Tilling Limited and Tilling & British Automobile Traction Limited.

At various dates in the first year, a host of independent companies was taken over. They were: G. H. Allitt & Sons Limited, Amersham & District Motor Bus & Haulage Ltd., B.B.P. Omnibus Co. Ltd., Birch Bros. Ltd., E. Brickwood Limited, Cardinal Omnibus Co. Ltd., Chariot Omnibus Services Limited, Cleveland Omnibus Co. Ltd., Convey & Clayton, Eagle Omnibus Co. Ltd., Earl Motor Omnibus Co. Ltd., Empress Motors Limited, Enterprise Transport Co. Ltd., Essex Omnibus Co. Ltd., Filkins & Ainsworth Limited, Glen Omnibus Co. (London) Ltd., Gordon Omnibus Co. Ltd., Robert Hawkins & Co. Ltd., F. W. Hayes, Holliday & Bangs, E. G. Hope, F. J. C. Kirk, A. Mills, Nelson Omnibus Co. Ltd., Paterson Omnibus Co. Ltd., Peræque Transport Co. Ltd., C. H. Pickup, Pioneer Omnibus Company, Powell & Whybrow, Premier Omnibus Co. Ltd., Premier Line Limited, Pro Bono Publico Limited, E. Puttergill Limited, A. H.

Raper, F. A. Rasey, Red Rover Omnibus Limited, Renown Traction Co. Ltd., Charles Russett & Son, Ryan Omnibus Company, F. Steer, A. G. Summerskill Limited, Supreme Motor Omnibus Co. Ltd., Triumph Motor Omnibus Company, United Omnibus Co. Ltd., Woolvett & Carswell, Lewis Omnibus Co. Ltd.

A list of famous names indeed. Other well-known firms not taken over quite so quickly – because the finances took longer to sort out – were: Ambassador Bus Co. Ltd., Chocolate Express Omnibus Co. Ltd., City Motor Omnibus Co. Ltd., Miller Traction Co. Ltd., Perkins Omnibus Co. Ltd., Prince Omnibus Co. Ltd., Reliance Omnibus Co. Ltd., St. George Omnibus Co. Ltd., Sphere Omnibus Co. Ltd., Victory Omnibus Co. Ltd., and Westminster Omnibus Co. Ltd.

Also at the end of the first year the Board had acquired or taken steps to acquire 68 other bus and coach undertakings in the Aylesbury, Gravesend, Grays, Guildford, Romford, St. Albans, Slough, Staines, Ware, Watford, and Woking areas, and others were pending in Grays, Romford, and Slough.

The Act provided that operators of stage and express carriages on which passengers were carried local to the Special Area and who were in possession of road service licences current on 31 October 1933, should, if they wanted to continue such services after 1 January 1934, apply before 31 October 1933, to the Board for consent. Applications were received from 320 operators providing services mainly in connection with sightseeing tours, race meetings, football matches, and other events of an intermittent character. After reviewing the circumstances of each application, the Board gave consent to 251 operators to continue all the services for which they had applied (1,404) and partial consent to five operators to continue 54 services. It refused consent to 69 operators providing 129 services. By this action, the Board became liable either to take over the whole or part of the 129 services or to pay compensation for the restriction imposed.

At 30 June 1934, the Board had acquired the undertakings or parts of undertakings of 58 of these operators. Of the remaining 11 undertakings, five were in the process of acquisition and three were given limited consent to continue for a period. Three others were given full permission to continue, the Board's previous refusal of consent being withdrawn. Other operators were purchased later.

Part of the activities of certain 'provincial' companies were also taken over. These were the Aldershot & District Traction Co. Ltd., Eastern National Omnibus Co. Ltd., Maidstone & District Motor Services Limited, Redcar Services Limited, and Thames Valley Traction Co. Ltd.

The size of the problem confronting the new Board, which also had to weld the railways and trams into a single unit with the buses, can be gauged from the lists given above. Arrangements were also made with the main-line railways for a Standing Joint Committee to be set up, as well as the receipts pooling scheme for the L.P.T. Area required to be established by the Act. An agreement was concluded with the Associated Equipment Co. Ltd. (AEC) for the supply of bus chassis and spare parts for 10 years. The number of bodies built at Chiswick had to be no more than the average built during the previous five years.

At mid-1934, the L.P.T.B. had 34,148 staff for its Central buses, 5,891 for the country services, 19,558 for trams and trolleybuses, and 1,752 providing services for both road and rail activities (there were also 14,119 railwaymen).

The road rolling stock fleet consisted of 5,976 buses and coaches, 2,560 trams, and 61 trolleybuses, plus 542 lorries, vans, and miscellaneous road vehicles. The buses and coaches, in the first year, ran 258,199,086 miles in service and carried 1,950,467,346 passengers. There were 89 garages and 32 tram and trolleybus depots.

It is not the purpose of this book to worry the reader with statistics, but these few have been included to show the sheer enormous size of the Board's undertaking and the genius of Lord Ashfield and his administrative partner, Frank Pick, in giving it a corporate image and welding it into a single body with a single, recognizable – and soon much-respected – entity.

Various references have been made in this book to 'country' services and, since they now became part of the L.P.T.B., this is perhaps the place to say how they began – excluding the long-distance 'horse mails' to Barnet, Woodford, etc. taken over by the L.G.O.C. at its original inception. The L.G.O.C. did in fact continue as far as was practicable to maintain the country links it inherited and later developed new ones, particularly when reliable motor buses became available from 1910 onwards.

The development of bus routes within, rather than to and from, London's 'country areas' really began in the 1920s when, in particular, the L.G.O.C. in partnership with the National Omnibus & Transport Company (one of the Clarkson descendants) in the north and the East Surrey Traction Company in the south, did much in this direction. The agreement with the National was made on 21 July 1921; that with the East Surrey had been made 14 days earlier. A further agreement, this time with the Thames Valley Traction Company, was made from 20 April 1922. The National routes were worked, in general, by L.G.O.C. types of bus in L.G.O.C. colours, differing from central London buses only in the name on the side and sometimes minor modifications to meet local conditions. At first the route numbers were prefixed by an 'N', but after the 1924 Act this vanished and most routes were renumbered in the series from 300 onwards.

The East Surrey, founded by Arthur Henry Hawkins, was a more individual company. It had its headquarters at Bell Street in Reigate and worked an area stretching from Horsham to Croydon. The company was formed on 16 March 1911 and began working on May 23 a Reigate–Redhill route using two single-deck, 24-seater Leyland buses. The first working arrangement, at local level, was made with the L.G.O.C. in 1914 when the L.G.O.C. started a Stockwell–Merstham service which later continued to Reigate. The East Surrey grew over the years and its blue and cream buses spread over a wide area after the war. Although the East Surrey had many types of vehicles, a large proportion was made up of L.G.O.C. types and the L.G.O.C. colouring was adopted later. The route numbers had had 'S' prefixes, but from December 1924 were mainly numbered from 400 upwards. The L.G.O.C. acquired control of the East Surrey in May 1929 – it had already taken control of Autocar Services Ltd. of Tunbridge Wells in February 1928.

These and the National bus fleet were swept into London General Country Services Limited (the new name of the East Surrey) in 1932. The company, with A. H. Hawkins in charge, had its headquarters at Reigate and painted its buses red with the fleet name 'General Country Services' on the side. But the new company had only a short separate life – it was taken into the L.P.T.B. organization in 1933.

A number of express coach routes had been started in 1928 by various operators to meet the growing demand for fast services between central London and towns on the perimeter. The L.G.O.C. entered this field, too, and on 9 July 1930 Green Line Coaches Limited was incorporated as a private company with the L.G.O.C. holding all the issued capital. A. H. Hawkins was again managing director. The first service ran between Charing Cross and Guildford, but by 1934 there were 28 routes served by 250 'luxurious motor coaches of 95 horse-power each'. A. H. Hawkins continued as Operating Manager of Country Buses and Coaches under the L.P.T.B. until he retired in 1946.

On these foundations, an extensive network of country buses and coaches was to be built up in the years to come. The report for the year ended mid-1935 drew attention to the way in which the acquisition of under-

The London Transport Area in the early 1960s. The 'Greater London' boundary formed the approximate division between Central and Country bus operations

takings had made it possible to review the traffic requirements of an area as a whole, 'Out of a mass of unrelated and often conflicting services in the country areas, the Board have attempted to build a co-ordinated and regular system. In doing so they have sought to preserve every necessary public facility and to anticipate to some extent the future requirements of the travelling public'. Consolidation schemes for the Dartford, Gravesend, Grays, Hemel Hempstead, St. Albans, and Watford districts had already

[81]

been introduced and those for Amersham, Windsor, and elsewhere were in advanced stages. In the north-western and eastern parts of the Board's area co-ordination schemes had been introduced for the coach services.

Not so much change was needed in the central area where there was already a great measure of agreement on services, but some adjustments were made to tram workings and others to buses. Traffic was growing, and new and augmented bus services were needed to keep pace. The acquisition of many types of vehicles, some of which needed rare specialized knowledge to maintain them properly, also caused difficulties. The Board found itself with 40 types of chassis and many more types of bodies and it decided early on that all the miscellaneous vehicles must be replaced by standard types as soon as possible. In the first two years 779 new vehicles were introduced and the obsolete buses were withdrawn in stages, simplifying and improving maintenance and reducing costs.

From 25 February 1935 the maintenance of central and country buses and of coaches was put under a new department centred on Chiswick and standardized methods were introduced throughout the entire fleet. (A similar organization, based on Charlton Depot, was set up for the trams.) Garage accommodation was also taken in hand and a start was made on building new garages to replace old and inefficient ones – especially in the country area – and on enlarging the better ones on modern lines and providing all of them with up-to-date equipment.

Many miles of tram track were due for renewal and the Board decided to substitute trolleybuses for trams in these areas.

In January 1932 the Minister of Transport appointed a committee under Lord Amulree to inquire into the operation of motor coach services in London. The recommendations of the Amulree committee led to statutory orders which caused most of the coach routes to be diverted from central London to the outskirts and limited in the number of stopping places.

The result was a drop of more than 25 per cent. in the number of passengers carried on the Board's coaches.

During 1934 bus route numbers were rationalized to do away with variations for short workings or minor bifurcations and in 1935 the first system of 'compulsory' and request stops was introduced. This began as an experiment over the full length of the Euston Road–Tottenham (Seven Sisters Corner) route. It resulted in more regular services and was accepted by the public as a whole 'with no more than minor criticism'. The Board resolved to adopt it throughout the central area.

The 1936 report is interesting in being the first in which London Transport drew attention to the growth of private transport and the consequent effect of congestion on its road services and costs. Private transport also began to accentuate the difference between peak and off-peak traffic. Experience with trolleybuses decided the Board to proceed with the withdrawal of all tram routes and to substitute trolleybuses for them. 'The removal of the trams', said the report, 'improves the fluidity of the traffic on the streets and should, therefore, be beneficial to the bus and coach operations of the Board, for there is scarcely a street with a tramway which is not also served by one or both of these means of transport'.

The mid-1938 report set out the results of the Board's first five years of operations. It revealed that in those five years the Board had purchased 2,975 new buses – mainly to replace obsolete vehicles. This number represented very nearly half (47%) of the fleet. Another 397 buses and coaches were on order. A great deal of work had been done on the modernization of garages and Chiswick Works was being replanned and enlarged to deal with the 6,400 strong bus and coach fleet and allow room for future expansion. The record day's traffic came in 1935 when, in the main fortnight of the Silver Jubilee celebrations, 153 million passengers were carried by all the Board's services and on Saturday,

A six-wheel 'P1' type six-wheel trolleybus, photographed in March 1941

May 4, 14¼ millions. What might have been a similar result during the Coronation of 1937 was marred by a long strike – from May 1 to May 27 inclusive – of Central busmen, mainly over working hours. The fall in traffic caused by this strike was not recovered until the following spring. Receipts, numbers of passengers, and services of all kinds provided by the Board rose steadily in those years – as did working expenses, and already the Board was calling attention to the heavy burden placed upon it by various forms of taxation – especially in fuel tax and vehicle licensing fees.

In the following year the Board had to report that while there had been an increase in traffic the rate of growth had continued to decline and working expenses continued to rise. Jointly with the main-line railways, the Board made formal application for a fares increase, on 10 January 1939, to the Railway Rates Tribunal. The increases were not approved by the Tribunal until 24 May 1939 and the administrative work necessary to put the increases into force took a few days. The higher fares could not be charged until 11 June 1939. This long gap between the application for a fares increase and its implementation was to be typical of such applications for many years, resulting in severe losses of revenue, until at last a quicker procedure was devised which enabled the increases to have a closer impact on the situations which they had been designed to meet.

But now the war was at hand and air raid precautions and a general rush to complete such works as were possible was the order of the day. The Board, like other good employers, had encouraged its staff to join the territorial forces and in October 1938 it had been given permission to form its own territorial anti-aircraft regiment – the 84th (London Transport) Anti-Aircraft Regiment, Royal Artillery. It consisted of headquarters

A 'TF' type coach in Green Line livery, with running letters for Romford (London Road) garage

and four batteries, and was commanded by Lt.-Col. A. W. C. Richardson, D.S.O., one of the Board's senior officers.

Before we examine the part the buses played in the Second World War we will take a look at what sort of buses they were and the technical progress that had been made.

The most numerous type of bus in London during the Munich shadows and the approach to war was the 'STL', which, in its various forms had reached the 2,600 mark, with all but 600 or so fitted with oil engines. There were also more than 1,200 double-deck 'LT' buses and just over 200 single-deckers of the same class; well over 1,000 'ST' buses with variants bringing their full numbers to more than 1,100; more than 400 'T' type single-deckers of which 316 were modern vehicles built for the Green Line services and fitted with oil engines; more than 200 of the 'Q' type; 100 of the 'STD' type; nearly 100 single-deck 'C' type and eight 'C' type fitted with special bodies for inter-station working; and 49 'CR' type single-deckers.

Some of these types have not been men-tioned previously. The 'STD' buses were pur-chased in 1937 from Leyland's. They had the Leyland TD4 type chassis and the same manufacturer's 8.6-litre diesel engine. Even the bodies – all-metal – were built by Ley-land's but were adapted to resemble the body of the standard 'STL'. The final ten of the series originally had hydraulic torque con-verters – a type of drive which enabled the conventional gearbox and clutch to be elimi-nated; but after a year or so of experience in running, the torque converters were replaced by conventional transmission.

The 'C' type was based on the Leyland Cub chassis, a small four-wheel chassis with the driver placed behind the six-cylinder oil engine instead of in the forward position used for larger buses. They were introduced in 1935 and were arranged for operation by one man, although a conductor could be carried if required, and were meant for operation on routes where road conditions or the likely number of passengers made larger buses un-suitable. One-man operation meant the pro-vision of a forward entrance with a door under the control of the driver. The first of the 20-seat bodies was built at Chiswick, but the others were mainly built by Short Brothers or Metro-Cammell-Weymann.

The inter-station 'C' type buses were most unusual vehicles. They were specially-designed to take over, on behalf of the main-line railways, the inter-station workings which had previously been carried out by a contractor. They were on a petrol-engined Leyland Cub chassis with forward control and the bodies were built by Park Royal Coachworks. The rear seats were raised on a 'half-deck' – popularly known as the 'observation platform' – so that the space below could be used for the heavy luggage which railway passengers in those days always seemed to have with them.

The 'CR' class appeared in 1939 and was stored during the war, appearing again (to surprise many Londoners who did not know of their existence) as relief buses in 1946. These small buses were again based on the Leyland Cub chassis but took the next step on from the 'Q' class in having their engines at the rear, though mounted vertically, longitudinally on the centre line of the bus, instead of in the transverse position of rear engines today. They seated 20 and had forward entrances with power-operated sliding doors.

Another class not yet mentioned was the 'TF' which came into use in quantity – 75 of them – in 1939 as a Green Line coach after the first 12 (apart from the prototype) had been introduced as private-hire coaches with special curved glass panels in the roof and an opening top. The 'TF' class was far ahead of its time, having its horizontal 8.6-litre oil engine placed beneath the floor in the same manner as most coaches today. All but one of the private-hire coaches were lost when in 1940 a bomb fell on the Peckham garage where they were stored.

But we are anticipating. The story of the war is for the next chapter.

XII The Second World War

EVEN before Munich (1938) the L.P.T.B. had begun its planning against the probable effects of air raids and specially-equipped squads with their manuals of instructions and a comprehensive backing organization were made ready. Instructors were trained who in turn trained others. Other preparations were made in anticipation of a reduction in the mileage the buses would be able to run and methods of blacking out buses and premises were evolved. Conductors were trained to drive in case too many experienced drivers were taken into the forces and the possibilities of recruiting women, as in the First World War, to take the places of the men conductors were considered. Huge quantities of equipment, from sandbags and shovels to stirrup pumps and protective clothing, were purchased and stocked against need. In late September 1938 things looked so threatening that 1,500 men from the works at Chiswick, with their comrades from the railway overhaul works at Acton next door, were released from normal duties to dig trenches in which the staff could shelter from air raids.

The Home Office asked London Transport, in mid-1938, whether Green Line coaches could be swiftly adapted as ambulances if war came. Equipment was designed at Chiswick and sent out to the Green Line garages in September 1938. A few coaches were converted immediately on a 'trial run' basis. On 31 August 1939 Green Line coaches were withdrawn from service. Hundreds of the coaches were converted – something like 400 in all – and were changed over to ambulances and placed under the control of the Ministry of Health within five hours of receiving the order to convert.

In the last weekend of August 1939, three

London schoolchildren leave the capital in high spirits

complete anti-aircraft divisions had to be moved to war stations in various parts of the Home Counties. The move was made in 489 London buses. Territorials had to be moved from their local drill halls to quarters in various parts of London and the countryside around. Once again the London bus was called in and members of the Queen's Westminsters, the London Irish Rifles, the Middlesex Regiment, the East Surreys, the Essex Regiment, and the Royal West Kents, all took their first journey into war in the familiar London bus.

On September 1 blackout was imposed. London Transport had been ready for this for some time, and temporary paper kits – to be followed by slotted headlamp masks – and other equipment were ready for fitting to the buses. The Railway Executive Committee, of which Frank Pick was a member, was established on the same day (it had been in

'shadow' existence since Munich) to co-ordinate the activities of London Transport and the four main-line railways to the best effect during the war to come. Those activities began in earnest on the same day with the start of the long-planned evacuation of schoolchildren from London to places of comparative safety in the country. Some of the journeys were long and had to be made by double-deck bus, but the routes had been planned in advance to make sure that a double-decker driver in strange country on unfamiliar roads did not find himself running up to a bridge so low that it would have removed the roof of his bus.

The evacuation took four days and, apart from the longer journeys mentioned, London buses were heavily engaged on moving children from outlying railway stations to their final destinations. The Green Line coaches, in their ambulance role, took stretcher patients, eight or ten at a time, to railheads for evacuation and patients from Barts were taken direct by coach to the King Edward VII Hospital at Windsor. All the London Transport services – buses, trams, trolley-buses and trains – and the main-line railways, worked together as a team in this tremendous task. London Transport vehicles alone evacuated half a million people, mostly children.

While all this was going on the public at large still had to be carried, so that the remaining buses had to carry more people and to run special services to compensate as far as possible for the absence of all the buses engaged on the evacuation.*

Towards the end of this hectic period, on 3 September 1939, came the official announcement that the nation was at war. Within a very short time the bus staff had been depleted by some 2,500 Territorials, reservists, and others on whom the services had a call. Up to 100 buses were 'on call' to the police in case they were needed in emergency, although in fact the police rarely called on these buses in the course of the war. Buses which *were* called away were single-deckers allocated, with their drivers, to the London Fire Brigade to help in emergencies in provincial towns. The drivers went off in them with their bags packed, knowing they might not be back for some days. In the course of time these buses found themselves as far afield as Birmingham, Bristol, Coventry, Southampton, and Stockport.

A sudden cut of 25 per cent. in petrol and oil fuel meant the withdrawal of many buses from the road on 16 September 1939. Most of the routes chosen for the cuts were covered by other means of transport but, despite planning in expectation of such cuts, it was impossible to produce new bus schedules in the time allowed. A mileage reduction was brought in on September 23, the day on which branded petrol disappeared and wartime 'pool' petrol took its place.

* In the evacuation, 4,988 buses, 533 trams, and 377 trolleybuses were used, as well as 640 special Underground trains.

Two days after this a limited number of Green Line services were restored, using buses, and on September 27 the permitted number of standing passengers on road vehicles was raised from five to eight. The petrol cuts had taken 839 buses off the roads by January 1940 and other buses worked only in the peak hours. Other services were cut during the evening as once it became dark and the blackout was established there was little traffic offering. The total mileage saved by these means was about 30 per cent. Yet another call had been made on experienced drivers in November 1939 when more than 430 were released to the Army so that they could train drivers of military vehicles.

On the technical side a notable event occurred on 17 July 1939 when the first 'RT' bus entered service. The first chassis had in fact been working before with an 'ST' body. In this guise it ran from what is now Southall garage on route 18C from December 1938 to February 1939. It was then withdrawn and was brought back into use later with a specially-designed body built at Chiswick. Although the design of this new 55-seater double-deck bus was completed as early as 1937 it was a remarkably advanced vehicle with an AEC 9.6-litre oil engine and air-pressure operated pre-selective gearbox and brakes. The body was much smoother in outline than previous buses and the reduction in the number of lower-deck side windows to four instead of the usual five or six gave it an undeniable grace.

This first 'RT' was so successful that an order was placed for more and another 150 – this time with 56 seats – were delivered before wartime conditions made it impossible for more to be built. We shall return to the 'RT' after the war, when it was modified to some extent, but it is worth recording that as these words were being written, nearly 34 years after the first 'RT' chassis carried passengers, there were still over 1,500 of these buses serving Londoners. They are the last of some 7,000 'RT'-type buses – the largest class ever to run in London.

To return to the war. The period of quiet which followed the initial alarms of war led to some relaxations. The blackout in particular caused great operating difficulties and London Transport, with Government co-operation, evolved modified fittings which gave a better standard of lighting. These eventually became standard throughout the country. On 3 January 1940 buses with reading lights appeared on the streets for the first time and on January 17 more Green Line routes were restored, largely to help with peak traffic. Some 160 of the converted coaches were reconverted and restored for a time to Green Line services but they were withdrawn again in 1942. During 1940 these restorations were being made stage by stage. In April the Minister of Transport agreed to some relaxation of the severe cuts in bus services and these were reduced from the 30 per cent. then obtaining to 25 per cent.

In May the war suddenly sprang to shocking life and refugees from France, Holland, and Belgium began to flood into Britain. The flood grew to such proportions that on one day 812 buses were being used to meet refugee trains at the main-line stations and carry their passengers to reception and rest centres such as Alexandra Palace and the stadium at Wembley. Because of the invasion danger presented by the collapse of France, plans were made for the evacuation of towns along the Sussex and Kent coasts and also of Southend. No fewer than 530 double-deck and 20 single-deck London buses were earmarked to take part in this mass migration should it become necessary. Women and children were to go first and then the rest of the population, the evacuation to be completed within five days. Another 90 double-deckers were to be used to carry refugees from the south-east coastal areas under a separate scheme.

The London Transport Territorial anti-aircraft regiment has already been mentioned, but with the formation of the Local Defence Volunteers, as the Home Guard was originally called, many more London busmen and their fellows from the trams, trolleybuses, and Underground had a chance to volunteer. And volunteer they did, to the tune of six battalions, two of which were manned entirely by busmen. Later on it became necessary to reorganize on a more geographical basis and men from all sections of London Transport found themselves mounting guard together. They were no longer battalions of busman or railwaymen, but London Transport battalions – and eventually a seventh battalion was formed. Over 30,000 of the staff served in these units.

Dunkirk itself brought the Green Line ambulances into operation again and buses were used on emergency services to assist the railways, but in the aftermath of Dunkirk there was a second evacuation of schoolchildren, including some who had drifted back to London in the breathing spell Britain had so fortunately been granted. This second evacuation took place between June 13 and June 18, when most people were convinced that invasion was only weeks, at most, away. Only a week later came Central London's first genuine air raid 'alert'. This was in the small hours of the morning of June 25, but no bombs were dropped. The first bombs came on August 15 round Croydon Airport (causing casualties among London Transport staff on loan to an aircraft manufacturer to help in repairing the Spitfires and Hurricanes of the 'Few') and Central London's first baptism came on the night of August 24/25. This heralded a period which lasted until the end of the year with bombs falling almost every night.

In October busmen were issued with steel helmets and on the night of October 14/15, as though to emphasise the need for this measure, an enemy bomb scored a direct hit on London Transport's headquarters at 55 Broadway. Just the day before, a decision had been taken there to reduce the size and thickness of bus tickets. This apparently small contribution to the war effort was to save over 600 tons of woodpulp, with all the transport and processing connected with it, in a single year. Measures to salvage used tickets and obsolete

*A double-decker of Central S.M.T. Co. at Trafalgar Square, with St. Martin-in-the-Fields
church on the right. It was one of many provincial buses on loan to London*

stock, with other paper, resulted in a contribution of another 700 tons of pulp a year.

The shortage of manpower was beginning to make itself felt, so womanpower was mobilized to take its place. Women conductors appeared on trams and trolleybuses in October and on Central buses in November. They had been working on the country routes since July.

By October quite a number of buses had suffered from bombs – either directly, as when one fell on Northfleet garage, damaging 15 buses, but fortunately killing no-one, or from bomb splinters, or from the effects of damage done to roads by bombing. A bus found itself the target of machine-gun fire at Chaldon Crossroads on 18 August 1940. Many more buses had to run emergency services when bombs interrupted railway services – either by actual damage or by their unexploded presence on or near the line – and road craters forced others to operate on sometimes long diversions. Trolleybuses and trams were held up when their power supply

was cut or their track damaged. In these circumstances London Transport found itself short of buses. To quote the annual report for the 18 months to the end of 1940:

'Since September 1940, the chief problems have been, first to overcome the effects of air-raid damage to the Board's properties and to the roads traversed by the Board's vehicles and, secondly, to provide the concentration of transport necessary to get passengers home before darkness in the winter months. The Board had anticipated the possibility of intensive air raids on London, and had taken steps to establish emergency organizations to deal with their effects. In the Engineering Department a special organization has been developed to deal promptly with damage, and staff have been on duty continuously so that, in all but exceptional cases, repairs have been effected and services restored after comparatively short delays. In the Operating Department, also, a special organization had been established, which has had at its disposition an emergency fleet con-

One of the 'steamer buses', which ran as a wartime experiment for a short time between Westminster aud Woolwich in 1940. A London Transport conductor can be seen collecting the fares

sisting of roundly 600 double-deck buses, with a reserve of a further 300 buses. This fleet has been used to supplement or replace interrupted services on the suburban lines of the main-line railways, and the railway, tram and trolleybus systems of the Board. The earlier closing of business premises in the latter part of 1940 reduced the normal evening peak period of 2½ hours to about an hour, and buses from the emergency fleet, together with buses hired from other transport undertakings, were used to reinforce the normal services. . . .'

The hired buses – there were 472 in all – came from all over the country and even from Scotland. Nearly a hundred came from Manchester, but the first to begin running in London (on 23 October 1940) came from Halifax. There were buses of many colours and shapes – from Leeds and Exeter, from West Bridgford and Hull, from Inverness and Aberdeen. Some stayed in London for months, some were called back to meet emergencies in their own cities, as with the blitz on Birmingham. The last returned home in June 1941. A few trolleybuses, even, were borrowed – from Bournemouth.

Because the suburban railway services were so often interrupted, London Transport, as we have seen, frequently had to run emergency services. This seems to have given rise to the idea of 'express' bus services, duplicating busy ordinary routes, which would run non-stop over the 'trunk' sections of their journeys between London and the suburbs. Separate queues were formed for the express vehicles. The first 10 'express' routes began working on October 24 and, taking advantage of the comparative emptiness of the streets caused by private car petrol rationing, they gave good service. Ten more routes were similarly treated shortly afterwards.

London Transport, under its Act, had certain powers in relation to providing passenger services on the Thames, though these had never been exercised and there was no intention to use them. London Transport busmen, however, found themselves working on pas-

The price of war

senger vessels after all when, by arrangement with the Minister of Transport and the Port of London Authority (which provided the vessels and crews as the Board's agents), a service was begun on the river between Westminster and Woolwich, with stops at numerous piers, on 13 September 1940. Fifteen boats were used for the service with London Transport bus inspectors and conductors dealing with the fares and tickets. The service, intended as a supplementary means of reaching riverside factories and wharves, began after a particularly bad disruption of tram and trolleybus services in East London due to substation damage, which interrupted electricity supplies. Even so, after the first novelty, the length of time taken by the journey – 2hr. 22min. from end to end – caused a decline in traffic and the short-lived – though venturesome – experiment ceased on 2 November 1940, having twice been interrupted by mines in the river – an unusual hazard for busmen. While it ran it carried about 1,000 passengers a day.

It is no part of this book to quote 'war stories'. The subject has been covered in detail in London Transport's official account of the war years, *London Transport Carried On*, written by Charles Graves. Though long out of print, it can still be found in many libraries. That being said, there is space for one or two items to show what it was like. There was the Building Department man who said, 'When we were at Camberwell Garage there was bomb damage there and Jerry was knocking it down quicker than we could put it up.' And the bus driver who explained, 'My bus began prancing about like a horse and the next thing I knew was that I was lying in a shop doorway . . .'. After receiving first aid he went back to his bus, ' . . . but as I approached it I said to myself, 'Its O.K., somebody's moved it. But when I came nearer I saw to my horror that only the roof was protruding from the crater in the road'.

Perhaps the climax of this period was reached on the night of 29/30 December 1940 with the concentrated incendiary bomb raid on the City of London and the raging fires which followed. As far as London Transport was concerned the major damage was to its railway installations, but the trams also suffered. For the bus operators the following morning was a nightmare, with 656 buses engaged on running emergency services to cover the dislocated rail, tram, and trolleybus routes.

In the country area there was one cheerful note. The restoration of Green Line services – though often using buses instead of coaches – reached a stage on 18 December 1940 where the equivalent of prewar services was being run. In fact, however, there had been a considerable increase in traffic in the outer London area so that the restored capacity was badly needed.

Air raids continued, though not with such regularity. The worst night of all for London Transport was that of 10/11 May 1941, in which its properties and services received very severe damage. Hundreds of buses were put out of action and the blocking of roads and bridges made it almost impossible to run services the following day.

The eased conditions which followed the German attack on Russia in June 1941 and the switching of bombing away from Britain enabled gradual improvements to be made, though the shortage of supplies and the need for London Transport, through its workshops, to contribute in other ways to the war effort did not make the provision of material any easier. In November there appeared a single-deck bus converted to carry 20 standing passengers and on November 20 the regulations were changed to allow 12 standing passengers, instead of eight, to travel on buses.

At the end of November, London was able to repay the provinces for the loan of buses in time of need by sending the first of 334 to help in other hard-hit cities. Five of these buses went to Coventry, and in all they served 48 provincial operators. London itself at last received a few – just over 50 – new buses. These were made up of chassis which had been partially built by AEC, Leylands, and Bristol before production ceased. Some received new bodies which had also been 'frozen' and others had bodies built to a rigid specification laid down by the Ministry of Supply which allowed no frills. The first of these 'utility' austerity buses, an 'STD', went into service on 1 December 1941.

One week after this a Halifax bomber took to the air for the first time – one of many such bombers going into service. The special feature of this one was that it had been built by a group – London Aircraft Productions – of which Lord Ashfield was Chairman, as a result of a scheme set up in 1940 even before the Battle of Britain. London Transport's part was to build the centre section, install the engines and the front section of the fuselage, and finally to complete the erection of and test-fly the aircraft. The rear fuselage was made by Chryslers, the nose shell by Duple, the inner wings and tailplane by Express

1941—The first Halifax bombers, which London Transport workers helped to fashion, shown in aerial salute at Leavesden

Motor & Body Works, and the outer wings by Park Royal.

Because there was not enough room at Chiswick, where the headquarters of the newly-fledged aircraft builders was situated, the part-finished railway rolling-stock depot then under construction at Aldenham was completed and used for the purpose. Later a new factory at the Leavesden airfield was made available to London Aircraft Productions. Most of the skilled staff were London Transport engineers, though very few of them had ever dealt with aircraft before, and they had a team of 4,600 workers. They built Halifax bombers for the rest of the war, the last – the 710th – being delivered to the Royal Air Force on 16 April 1945. Appropriately, they named it 'London Pride'.*

Calls for further service restrictions were

* Some of the other war tasks accomplished by London Transport road and rail engineering works are described in *The Story of London's Underground*, also published by London Transport.

made by the Ministry of Transport, but the traffic was such that only small changes could be made. They included restrictions on late evening running (and, later, on Sunday morning services). There were other changes designed to save fuel, however, including the parking of buses in Central London during the day to save light running to garages – a scheme which continued until May 1946 – and the conversion of over 250 buses to run on producer gas. These latter buses hauled behind a two-wheeled trailer on which the gas was produced from anthracite and water. The trailer had an anthracite hopper and firebox, a water-tank, and cooling equipment. Those who had anything to do with them speak of the peculiar smell which hung about them. The gas was a fairly efficient fuel, but the buses which used it were sluggish runners and bad on hills. Of the buses converted – and they were less than half of the 550 which the Ministry had directed should be changed – probably no more than 150 or so actually

A party of London Transport workers return to work after inspecting one of the last Halifax bombers which they helped to build

ran on gas. Those which did used a ton of anthracite a week and needed refuelling (usually by changing trailers at a garage) about every 80 miles.

Because of further fuel restrictions, Green Line coaches were again withdrawn on 29 September 1942 and the following week the Ministry of War Transport announced still more travel restrictions. Cheap travel tickets were withdrawn and the era of 'Is your journey really necessary?' was at hand. Nearly a hundred of the released Green Line coaches – oil-engined 'T' types – were handed to the American forces the following year for use as troop carriers and American Red Cross mobile canteens (Clubmobiles). Most of these came back to London Transport and were re-converted for use as Green Line coaches again when services were resumed in 1946.

Other events in 1942 included the Ministry of War Transport order making queueing compulsory from April 12; the adoption of fixed stops throughout Central London and in the larger towns in the country area, and the adoption of a new wartime colour – officially 'oxide red' – for the Board's road vehicles. The manufacture of new buses, to a wartime specification, was permitted in small quantities from 1942. London Transport put the first of these into service in December 1942. In all, 435 Guy chassis, with bodies by several manufacturers, were purchased for use in London, as well as 181 Daimlers, the first of which began work on 6 May 1944, and 20 Bristols, the first of which appeared on the roads in May 1943.

Even before 'D-Day' London Transport had been planning for its part in it, and on

June 2 London buses began moving troops from the London area right to the ships which were to take them across the Channel. Troop-carrying continued until July 4.

On 13 June 1944, a week after 'D-Day', the first 'V1' flying bomb fell in Southern England. On September 8 the first 'V2' rocket fell in London – at Chiswick – and the last landed at Orpington on 27 March 1945, to be followed the next day by the last two 'V1' flying bombs at Sidcup and Waltham Cross. Compared with the earlier bombing, the 'V1' and 'V2' attacks had little effect on London Transport services, although property was badly damaged in 270 incidents in the first three months or so of the 'V1' raids. In one incident, on 18 July 1944, Elmers End Garage received a direct hit. Sixteen people, including 10 busmen, were killed, 29 buses and 10 ambulances were put out of action, and buildings were badly damaged by the explosion and subsequent fires. Despite this, by miracles of improvization, the full bus service was operated from the garage the next day. The 'V2' rockets were expected to be a very serious menace and plans were drawn up accordingly, but although garages were damaged, none received a direct hit from a 'V2' and, by comparison with the earlier bombing raids, few buses were seriously damaged.

'VE' day came on 8 May 1945, and by then thoughts were already on the postwar period. The removal of the netting which had covered the windows of the wartime buses in the next few weeks was a symbolic act. Although the war still raged in the East, London now had to face the peace.

XIII Swings and Roundabouts

THE end of the war brought with it some difficult problems. The whole population and its living and work patterns had been disturbed for some years and all kinds of artificial restrictions and duties had been placed on transport. London Transport's task now was to estimate what calls on its services peacetime would be likely to impose. It was fortunate in having survived the war with most of its system intact and a higher level of demand for transport than in prewar days. But how much of this demand was temporary? What of the higher cost of all supplies and the cost of replacing the ageing bus fleet? What would be the attitude of the staff after years of war and what improvements would have to be made in wages and conditions? Many of these problems were not for London Transport to answer alone – they affected the country as a whole – but some sort of temporary working answer had to be found just so that the organization could continue to run from day to day and month to month.

The return of men from the forces and the end of the war in the East, with a cessation of special war work in the maintenance shops, eased the staff position. More fuel became available and in July 1945 the first steps were taken to increase service levels, including Sunday morning services on 18 routes. By the end of the year many services had been restored and 700,000 more miles a week were being run on Central routes and 86,000 more on Country than 12 months earlier.

Very early came a staff dispute about the number of standing passengers allowed. New regulations reduced the number from 12 to eight and it was agreed that the number should drop to the prewar five by May 1946. There were also claims for improvements in pay and conditions from practically the whole of the staff.

The Board saw as its immediate objectives the full restoration of services; the replacement of older buses by an improved version of the 'RT' and of coaches by a new vehicle of advanced design; the restoration of vehicles generally to at least prewar standards of comfort, cleanliness, appearance, and mechanical efficiency; and endeavours to improve the standard of fare collection by using 'Pay-as-you-board' methods. The new emphasis on town and country planning which had emerged in the latter years of the war, reinforced by the Barlow Report (Report of the Royal Commission on the Geographical Distribution of the Industrial Population) and the County of London and Greater London Plans which followed as a result, put a new factor to work. Even in its 1945 report, seeing what could lie ahead, London Transport put in a plea that the bus should not be discriminated against in favour of the private car in any planning schemes and declared, 'Any attempt to deprive the bus of access to points to and from which there is a heavy traffic movement would not be in the public interest'. It is a theme which London Transport is still having to repeat today.

The 'Pay-as-you-board' experiment mentioned in the previous paragraph was carried out with two trolleybuses and three double-deck buses as a test before ordering new buses. An 'STL' bus was rebuilt with a combined centre entrance/exit and a power-operated sliding door worked by the conductor. The conductor was seated at a desk opposite the doorway. When the bus stopped he opened the door to let passengers off. Waiting passengers then boarded and filed past his desk to buy their tickets, which he issued from a cash-register type machine. The space in front of the desk would hold eight passengers, so that the door could be shut and there was normally no delay to the bus, which ran between Ealing and Hook on route 65 bearing a large 'PAY AS YOU BOARD BUS' notice.

Another 'STL' was given a forward entrance and centre exit with pneumatically-operated sliding doors under the control of the conductor, who sat at a desk inside the

entrance and was provided with ticket-issuing and change machines. The passenger 'reservoir' at the entrance had room for 12 to stand and was fitted with four tip-up seats to make up in some measure for the reduced number of fixed seats (18) on the lower deck. With these tip-up seats the normal 56-seat capacity was reduced by only two. Other experiments were made with doors fitted to a trolleybus and an 'RT' – both at the normal rear platform position, and a trolleybus fitted with a double centre door. The vehicles were tried out under various conditions but the Board concluded that the 'Pay-as-you-board' system was not suited to a fares system based on charges according to distance travelled. In all cases boarding time was found to be increased and there were other disadvantages which counteracted what improvements there were in fare-collection efficiency.

In 1946 traffic reached record heights and the increased population of London's country made particularly heavy demands on the country services. Green Line services were restored, the first on February 6 and the last on June 26.

The shortage of buses was causing concern at this time. Every available vehicle was being used despite the delivery of the last 69 of the 'utility' buses. Of 746 new buses ordered for delivery in 1946 only 225 arrived because of shortage of labour and supplies in the builders' factories. Those outstanding included 500 of the improved 'RT' type, of which another 500 were ordered in 1946 with an option for another 1,500. Many of these new buses were needed, for it had been decided that the remaining trams would be replaced with 'RT' buses and not trolleybuses since the latter, in postwar conditions, no longer had any appreciable economic advantages and required the upkeep of extensive electrical installations – and the war had demonstrated the value of the flexibility of the oil-engined bus.

The improved 'RT' chassis was built by AEC, complete interchangeability of parts being ensured by the methods of manufacture, but the bodies were built by two main manufacturers – Park Royal and Weymann's. It was considered essential that body parts should be equally interchangeable – the new maintenance methods were to depend on this – so a lesson was taken from wartime aircraft building experience and the manu-

was still used. Spring fillings and leather were used for the seats until rubber and moquette again became available. Great care was taken to make conditions for the crew as good as they could possibly be and special attention was paid, with numerous mock-up tests, to the driver's field of vision. Braking was highly

'RT' type bus on Route 12 at Oxford Circus

facturers worked to identical drawings, templates, and limits, and assembled parts on precisely similar jigs.

The postwar 'RT' chassis was known as the AEC Regent Mark III and had a 9.6-litre oil engine developing 120 b.h.p. at 1,800 r.p.m. Transmission was via a fluid flywheel and pre-selective gearbox operated by air pressure as were the brakes. Considerable use was made of metal in the body but some wood

efficient, with lighter pedal pressure, and the suspension was designed to give smooth riding almost indefinitely. Time has proved the quality of both bus and design.

By the end of 1947 some 4,000 'RT' double-deck buses were on order, but only 182 of them had been delivered. The whole of the year was a struggle to keep London's buses running in the face of the shortage of new buses and a large-scale breakdown in the

[97]

supply of spare parts. The Chief Mechanical Engineer (Road Services), A. A. M. Durrant, described it in October as 'the gravest crisis which London Transport has ever had to meet during its history'. 'It was', he declared, 'touch and go whether the service could be maintained.' Hundreds of buses were lined up in London Transport's works and elsewhere because there were no spare parts with which to repair them. London Transport men scoured the country for spare parts, even taking unfinished parts from the manufacturers for completion at Chiswick, which was already manufacturing heavy parts which normally called for specialized factories and equipment. Buses were 'cannibalized' so that parts from one bus might make half-a-dozen others roadworthy. And meantime the roadside queues grew . . . and grew. The number of road passengers travelling daily had increased from 9,070,000 in 1938/39 to 10,160,000 – and they were making longer journeys.

To meet the situation the Board hired vehicles. Between 1947 and 1950 something like 550 coaches were hired for 'L.P.T.B. Relief' services and nearly 200 buses were hired from the Tilling Group. The flood of 'RT' deliveries during 1949 and 1950 retrieved the position and the tram replacement programme could be begun. In 1952 it was finished and that year also the first single-deck 'RF' buses, built to the new dimensions of 30ft. length and 8ft. width authorized in 1950 were delivered. After the first 15 coaches had been built, however, the width was reduced to 7ft. 6in. for the remaining vehicles. The whole of the postwar programme of bus replacement was completed by 1954. By that time the Board had received 6,803 'RT'-type double-deck buses and 700 'RF' buses and coaches. The last 30 of the long-lived 'T' type had been received by Country buses in 1948. Among the new single-deck buses were 84 of the 'GS' type designed for London Transport on a Guy chassis, with bodies by Eastern Coachworks. They seated 26 and were normally operated by one man. The first appeared in October 1953.

Although resembling the 'RT' with AEC chassis in nearly every way, including interchangeable bodies, 1,631 'RT' buses were built on Leyland P.D.2 chassis with Leyland engines, but they incorporated the AEC type of transmission. These were classified 'RTL'. The possibility of using 8ft. wide bodies led to the ordering of 500 of this type of bus with bodies of that width. The bodies were built by Leyland to its own construction methods but closely to resemble the 'RT'. Because of their width they were at first confined to suburban routes, but later they were allowed into Central London. They were classified 'RTW' for fairly obvious reasons.

The letters 'RT' have given rise to much controversy and there are several possible explanations for them. The simplest, however, seems to be that the bus was on a Regent Mk. III chassis, or 'Regent Three', although there is also a good case for Regen T'.

As a background to all this, London Transport had found itself changed. Government control should have ended after the war – after allowing an 'unscrambling' period – but before this could happen the Transport Act of 1947 created the British Transport Commission and on 1 January 1948, when the Act came into force, the London Passenger Transport Board had ceased to exist and all its responsibliities had become those of the new London Transport Executive – one of the Executives of the B.T.C.

Although of great importance in the history of transport, the change made very little difference to the day-to-day working of London's buses or to policies on road transport. The tramway conversion scheme was carried out as planned and was completed in eight stages, the last trams being withdrawn on the night of 5/6 July 1952.

All London buses now had oil engines, the final runs of petrol-engined buses being made in the early morning of 21 November 1950 when the all-night 'inter-station' buses, which had been reinstated after the war, returned to their garages, leaving the fleet of some 7,500 buses and coaches to run on oil only. It was almost exactly 20 years since the first experiments with oil engines and 16 years – because of the war – since the decision to change over had been made. The noise problem was still present, but London Transport was concentrating on this by the use of the 'pilot injection' system which, whilst reducing engine noise, gave rise to maintenance troubles and was subsequently abandoned. The 'one-and-a-half-deck' Leyland Cub inter-station buses were replaced by ordinary 'RT' double-deckers. The economy of oil engines is shown by consumption in 1949 – the last year in which London Transport ran a reasonable number of petrol-engined buses. They averaged 5.07 m.p.g. against the 9.89 m.p.g. of the oil-engined buses, many of which were of prewar design.

Mention has been made in passing of the 'RF' buses and coaches. These were ordered to replace, in two years, the whole of the pre-war fleet of single-deck buses and coaches. The 'RF' vehicles were all of one basic design with underfloor engine and entrance forward of the front wheels. In many ways the general outline and appearance followed the lines of the 1932 'Q' type single-deck bus while the chassis arrangement was very similar to that of the 'TF' coach with which London Transport pioneered the underfloor engine as far back as 1937. As usual, special attention was paid in the design to ease of maintenance and as far as possible standard 'RT' components were incorporated.

The 'RF' order was for 700 vehicles more or less equally split between Central, Country, and Green Line services. The Central and Country buses both seated 41, the main difference being that the Country buses were fitted with power-operated folding doors. The Green Line coaches had only 39 seats but were fitted with luggage racks and a heating system. The first of the 'RF' coaches began work on 1 October 1951 on route 704 between Windsor and Tunbridge Wells, and the first Central bus went into service on route 210 (Finsbury Park–Golders Green) on

11 September 1952. They had AEC Regal Mk. IV chassis with the AEC 9.6-litre engine with fluid flywheel and pre-selective gearbox and 30ft. x 7ft. 6in. bodies by Metro-Cammell.

As already mentioned, a number of 'RF' coaches were built with 8ft. wide bodies for private hire and long-distance coach work. These were additional to the order for 700. They were classified as 'RFW' and had glazed roof panels and opening roofs.

With these new buses and coaches, the green Country fleet was to consist of roughly 800 'RT' double-deckers, 50 'RLH' 'low-bridge' double-deckers (special low-height bodies by Weymann on AEC Regent Mk. III chassis for routes with low bridges – dating from 1950), 500 single-deck 'RF' buses and coaches, and 60 one-man-operated buses (Leyland Cubs), with a few 'T' and 'STL' types.

Mention must be made here of the remarkable career of RT97, which was a normal 'RT' until badly damaged by a 'V1' in July 1944. It was rebuilt with air-operated sliding doors to the rear platform and used on route 65 in the 'Pay-as-you-board' experiments already mentioned, being then painted green and used for similar experiments on route 721. It then became a guinea-pig until it emerged in new glory in 1949 as RTC1, 'the world's most advanced public road vehicle'. It was in fact altered out of all recognition as an 'RT' with a new streamlined front with a chromium 'mouth-organ' grille. The radiator was placed under the stairs and linked with an automatic air-warming and ventilation system which changed the air $17\frac{1}{2}$ times an hour. The conductor had a seat beside the pneumatically-operated doors and the 46 passengers had 'air-liner type "sink-in" seats' tilted back, after many tests with volunteer passengers, six degrees more than those on ordinary buses. There was fluorescent lighting, the floors were covered with ripple rubber and the windows were given a painted surround to give a 'continuous' effect. It embodied many new patents, including those

A bus body being lifted from its chassis by overhead hoists

on the heating system – which could be reversed in summer to draw in cooler air from outside. It was finished in a new shade of green and had an illuminated Green Line sign. It was tried out on many routes to test passenger reaction and from it many lessons were learned which are still of value today.

engineering and aircraft works. The re-organization was well in hand at the time of the maintenance crisis already described but Chiswick alone could not cope with all the work. Because of this, what was described at the time as a 'baby Chiswick' was opened at the Aldenham depot which had been used for

'RM' type (Routemaster) bus on Route 37, seen here crossing Richmond Bridge

All the new buses were designed for new maintenance methods taking advantage of standardization, and Chiswick works went through a five-year re-organization to fit it for its new task. The original conception of Chiswick was perfectly sound but the re-organization was based on the latest available ideas from industry, including the production methods used in car factories and those which had been found of advantage in wartime

aircraft production. It came into full use in April 1949 and all postwar buses were sent there for repairs. Newly-delivered vehicles went straight to Aldenham to be fitted with destination blinds, fare boards, advertisements, etc. and were finally inspected and licensed for public service there. In fact, Aldenham was never required for the railway purposes for which it was originally built – largely because of the 'Green Belt' set up in its vicinity which took away the traffic potential for which the railway was being built. Aldenham continued in use as a bus overhaul works and in 1956 was re-equipped to deal with the repair of all bus bodies and frames in the London Transport fleet – in the region of 8,000, plus up to 2,000 more buses which were expected to enter the fleet as a result of the trolleybus conversion. Chiswick was again re-organized and from then on dealt only with the reconditioning of engines and mechanical and electrical units – as well as retaining its important development work on new bus designs.

Much work had also been done at the garages. In 1948 a programme of 'raising the roof' began at 45 bus garages to accommodate 'RT' buses, the first being Old Kent Road and Hammersmith. The roofs, weighing between 200 and 400 tons, were raised the necessary 9 or 10 inches in one piece by jacking them up, complete with parapet, building new brickwork in the gap created, and bedding the roofs down again. A standardized layout, adaptable to local conditions, was evolved for new garages. It incorporated a completely enclosed heated and ventilated docking area with improved pits, many of which communicated by a sunken workshop area, buses passing over the gap when moving over or off the pits by using bridging pieces. As a consequence of the South London tram conversion, many tram depots were reconstructed to take buses – involving filling-in the many pits characteristic of tram depots – and in 1950 new garages were begun at Stockwell – a remarkable piece of garage architecture – and at Rye Lane, Peckham.

On the traffic side there were innovations. 'Beauty Spot Limited' tours were introduced on Sundays, Saturdays, and Wednesdays in the summer of 1950, with a total of 39 wholeday, afternoon, or evening trips. Seats could be booked in advance at local garages. The most popular destinations were Whipsnade Zoo, Windsor, and Hampton Court, but there were also tours of the Surrey and Chiltern hills, the North Kent countryside and elsewhere, as well as visits to London Airport, Chessington Zoo, Penshurst, and Burnham Beeches.

People who went out for the day by ordinary services were not neglected. Radio control for buses was first tried at Epsom Races in 1948 and was then extended to weekend use at popular destinations such as Box Hill, Ranmore Common, and the Tillingbourne Valley. A radio van would tour bus stops in the areas concerned and when queues were seen to be building up a radio message was sent to Dorking bus station and a relief vehicle was sent on its way.

By 1950 London Transport had a new problem. It had all – or nearly all – the buses it required, but not enough men. A recruiting drive was begun in which the age for conductors was lowered to $19\frac{1}{2}$ and the upper limit for both drivers and conductors was raised to 50. This shortage of manpower was to be a recurrent theme, becoming more and more urgent as time went on. But that year was not all gloom. The Festival of Britain was on the horizon and four 'RT' buses toured Belgium, Denmark, France, Germany, Holland, Luxembourg, Norway, and Sweden to advertise it in advance. The Festival itself, in 1951, brought many more people into London to use London Transport services and special coach tours were arranged, with eight itineraries, for the tourists. In the same year, so that services could be properly coordinated, the Eastern National Company's local services in the Grays and Tilbury areas, with its Grays garage, were transferred to London Transport. The re-organized routes came into operation on 2 January 1952.

Another important change in these early 1950s was the introduction of what is now the familiar Gibson ticket machine with its 'instant printing' instead of the Bell Punch system which had been in use since 1893. The changeover was gradual, but the mechanization of ticket issues with Gibson or other machines had been completed by 1958. The Gibson machine was invented by George Gibson, a former superintendent of what is now London Transport's ticket-machine works.

In July 1953, A. T. Lennox-Boyd, then Minister of Transport, set up a Committee of Inquiry 'to inquire into the conduct of the undertaking carried on by the London Transport Executive . . . with a view to ascertaining what practical measures can be taken by the British Transport Commission and the Executive in order to secure greater efficiency or economy . . . '. Fares, being under the adjudication of the Transport Tribunal, were excluded from the inquiry. At the end of that year London Transport had 7,201 double-deck buses, 893 single-deck buses, 372 coaches, and 1,797 trolleybuses. Vehicle-miles run during that year were: Central buses 279 million, trolleybuses 74.2 million, country buses 47.9 million, and Green Line coaches 23.4 million. No fewer than 3,658 million passenger journeys were made on the road services during the year. When the Underground figures were added, they were the highest figures for any city passenger transport system in the world.

The committee (known as the 'Chambers Committee' after its chairman S. P. Chambers) received written evidence from 50 local authorities and other bodies and 130 members of the public, supplemented by oral evidence as required. In its report, issued in 1955, the committee stated: 'Comparatively few of the representations made to us indicated any serious dissatisfaction with the general quality of the services provided by the London Transport Executive.' It concluded that the undertaking was conducted efficiently and with due regard to economy but thought that efficiency could be improved and economies achieved if various measures – some of the most important of them outside the control of London Transport – could be put into force. The measures were all the more important 'because of the unsatisfactory financial position of the undertaking'.

Among the points made were the need to stagger hours and so to reduce transport costs by not having to use a very large fleet in peak hours which could only be under-employed for the rest of the day, and the need to alleviate street congestion and make stronger car parking and waiting restrictions. Special flat-fare short-journey peak-hour services, possibly using single-deck 'standee' buses, between focal traffic points such as railway stations and other major traffic objectives, were among the committee's suggestions. They did not consider 'standee' buses (i.e. buses with a high proportion of standing passengers) were suitable for other routes in London, nor did they think one-man-operation suitable except for certain country routes. Maintenance costs were considered too high and the numbers employed on the work excessive, but it was also considered that the standards demanded by the certifying officers and vehicle examiners of the Ministry of Transport were too meticulous. The scheduling of bus services and duty rosters was considered too inflexible. The decision, recently taken, to replace the trolleybuses by oil-engined buses was considered correct. The general standard of efficiency and conduct of bus crews was considered high but the general impression could be spoilt 'by the attitude of a small minority'.

The full report makes interesting reading, but the general picture is one of a mostly clean sheet with a few bad marks here and there.

To replace the trolleybuses, a double-deck bus of entirely new design was evolved under the direction of A. A. M. Durrant. It was intended to give standards of performance higher than anything that had been achieved before for buses or trolleybuses. No chassis was to be used, the main load-carrying member being the high-duty aluminium alloy body structure itself. A new form of coil springing with independent front and rear suspension was used. Small sub-frames were used on which to mount the mechanical units at front and rear. The AEC 9.6-litre engine, with a fluid flywheel and fully-automatic gearbox, together with hydraulic brakes, made driving simple and physical effort was relieved by the introduction of power-assisted steering. The new bus was developed by London Transport in conjunction with AEC and Park Royal. The result was a two-axled vehicle with seats for 64, of all-metal construction, with a saloon heating and ventilating system built into the design, 27ft. 6in. long and 8ft. wide, with an empty weight of under $7\frac{1}{4}$ tons and a laden weight, with passengers, crew, fuel, oil, and water, of about $11\frac{1}{2}$ tons. The original prototype appeared at the 1954 Commercial Vehicle Exhibition and aroused great interest. It was known as the 'Routemaster' or 'RM'.

Three other prototypes were built and run in passenger service. RM2 had AEC mechanical units and a body built by London Transport with assistance from Park Royal. RML3 had mechanical units by Leyland Motors Limited and a body by Weymann's, and CRL4 – built as a double-deck Green Line coach – had Leyland mechanical units and a body by Eastern Coach Works.

The first production model Routemaster, RM8, was shown at the Commercial Vehicle Exhibition in 1958, and the first three production models to run in passenger service, RM5, 7, and 24, operated on route 8 from Willesden Garage on 6 June 1959, followed by RM14 on route 11 from Riverside Garage six days later. The production vehicles have a somewhat different frontal appearance from that of the prototypes and differ in a number of details from them as a result of changes in legislation and of operational experience gained with the original vehicles.

Surprise was sometimes expressed that a bus which had 'started from scratch' should have its engine at the front and platform, without doors, at the rear, but opinion at the time was that a rear-engined bus was the best for London conditions.

In 1954 congestion was seriously affecting the bus services and a special team of road officials was brought together, after operational research had shown the need, to concentrate on bus services particularly affected by congestion and, out on the road, to adjust the position of buses in relation to others on the route to restore regularity as quickly as possible. But congestion, already well over a century old, was to get worse. Traffic carried by London Transport was growing before the war, and it grew after the war, but with the de-rationing of petrol in 1950 the trend changed. Between that year and 1955 the number of passengers fell by 10 per cent., the fall being mainly at weekends and in the evenings when profitability was highest. Although private cars, motor cycles, and 'scooters' probably accounted for much of the fall, the steady spread of television which kept people at home in the evenings instead of going out for their entertainment was a growing factor which was eventually to make the London suburbs 'cities of the dead' during the evenings, as one observer described them. Not only that, but shortage of staff was troubling the road services more and more severely. Despite rest day working and overtime by the staff, at some periods $5\frac{1}{2}$–6 per cent. of the scheduled mileage could not be operated. The irregularity thus created in the services was another factor which drove more people towards using their own transport – creating more congestion and worsening the bus services and turning more people to their own transport and so on in a tightening spiral damaging to environment and social life alike.

In 1955 London Transport was still earning a substantial working profit – £5 million – but it was not enough to meet its share of the central charges of the British Transport Commission – at that time £5.5 million. The cost of running the Commission's headquarters organization and the services common to the various sections of its undertaking, as well as the sums needed to pay interest on B.T.C. stock, were calculated annually and a suitable proportion of the total had to be found by each constituent undertaking, including London Transport. These sums were known as the 'central charges'.

The Green Line services, with their speed and private-car comfort, continued to grow

A 'B.E.S.I.' controller at work before his console

in popularity but were beginning to be affected by Central London congestion.

The year 1956 saw some improvement in the staff position but the general fall in passengers on the road services continued, even affecting the hitherto buoyant Green Line services, which were also to suffer in north and east London from the effects of competition from the new electrified services of British Rail's Eastern Region. At the end of the year there was a remarkable demonstration of the effect congestion was having on the bus services. With the Suez crisis came petrol rationing and a marked reduction in the number of cars running or parked in the streets. Although London Transport itself had a 5 per cent. cut in fuel supplies, the remaining buses were able to go about their work at higher speed and with greater regularity and to carry all the passengers offering – including the private motorists who had left their cars at home.

But reductions in scheduled mileages were being made as traffic fell. London Transport could not, if it were to pay its way, continue to run buses for which there was no demand. Though reductions were always made *after* the traffic fell and not before, the resultant worsening of the services in turn caused other would-be passengers to turn to other means of transport. There was no escaping the spiral. Aldenham was formally opened for bus body overhauls in that year, designed to service a fleet of nearly 10,000 vehicles, but already the signs of decline were there, even if not then acknowledged as permanent.

A bright moment came with 'London Bus Week' from 16 to 21 July 1956 in celebration of the centenary of the founding of the L.G.O.C. On the Monday morning there was a parade of historic buses in Regent's Park, including the new Routemaster as the representative of the latest buses. The parade was attended by the Minister of Transport and representatives of many transport undertakings from abroad.

[105]

XIV Change–but not Decay

IN 1957 London Transport paid its way, meeting all its operating costs and the minimum amount of the B.T.C. central charges applicable to it for the first time since 1948. The reason, admittedly, was the Suez petrol rationing, but it served to show what buses, given a reasonable chance, could do. But passenger traffic continued to fall and the continued concentration of peak hour travel, especially in the evenings, into shorter and shorter periods gave some cause for alarm. London Transport urged employers to support the Ministry of Transport's staggered hours campaign.

The effects of congestion continued despite the introduction of parking meters in 1958 but London Transport itself made a determined attack on the problem with the traffic squads of its bus running control, mentioned earlier, and with a prototype 'electronic eye' known fondly as 'B.E.S.I.' These initials (pronounced 'Bessie') stood for 'Bus Electronic Scanning Indicator'. It worked by having a number of fixed 'scanners' along a route which were able to 'read' a plate attached to the side of every bus on a route. Coded impulses from the reading head were sent back to a central control point over land lines and made to actuate a display which showed the route controller which section of a route held any given bus at any time. He could then tell at once where and when congestion was building up and arrange for an inspector to be sent to that section of the route to regulate the service, turning buses if necessary to get back to normal regular running. 'B.E.S.I.' has been improved over the years but still applies only to a small number of routes. It is likely to be overtaken by more modern methods of observation.

Another measure was 'route localization' in which a route passing through the central area might be reorganized so that buses ran at each end from the suburbs into the edge of the centre. Others would run across the centre and just into the suburban fringes. In this way the suburban sections were kept free of the worst effects of congestion and those in the centre only were affected. Some buses continued to cover the whole route for the sake of through passengers – but the majority of London bus passengers have always travelled short distances. Unfortunately this measure needed more buses as well as suitable turning points – which were not always there!

The main event of 1958 was the bus strike which lasted from May 5 to June 20 – the first to receive official trade union backing since 1937. This is not the place to argue the rights and wrongs of the strike but there can be little doubt, looking back over the years, that it was responsible for hastening the decline of the London bus services.

Work began in 1958 on the conversion of the trolleybus depots for bus operation, the first being Bexleyheath and Carshalton in March, followed by Poplar, Clapton, and Bow later in the year. Work was also put in hand on designing the new routes to be operated in the trolleybus areas once the constricting factor of the overhead power equipment was removed and the new buses could be 'tied-in' with the main bus network.

One-man operation, restricted at first to very small buses, had been tried with success on the single-deck routes of the country area. Although passengers sometimes took longer to board, one-man operation seemed not to affect the use made of the services and the system was extended to the larger 'RF' vehicles. By 1959, 189 one-man buses were running on the country services, in some cases replacing former crew-operated double-deckers. At the end of that year only three single-deck crew-operated country routes remained.

Little has so far been said about trolley-

A Routemaster bus, fitted with a special plate above the driver's cab on the nearside, passing a roadside 'B.E.S.I.' scanner, which transmits the information on the plate back to a central control office, thus identifying the bus and reporting its position on the route

buses in this book because they have been regarded in the old sense of 'trackless trams' rather than buses, but conversion to buses was in full swing in 1960 and a note on them would not be out of place.

On 16 May 1931 London United Tramways introduced its first trolleybus service between Twickenham and Teddington in south-west London. Within four months, the system had been extended to some 17 route miles on four routes in the Twickenham/ Kingston/Wimbledon area worked by 60 three-axle 56-seat double-deck trolleybuses, which later became known, for no very clear reason, as 'Diddlers'. One likely suggestion is that whereas trams kept to a straight and predictable course guided by their rails, the new trolleybuses 'diddled about all over the road'.

The four routes had been converted from electric tramways, of which London United had been the pioneer in London, as part of the company's policy of modernization and improvement. Several of the converted tram routes were short, some were laid in narrow streets, and all were served by trams which were 24 or more years old.

When the London Passenger Transport Board was formed in July 1933 it absorbed the London United's tram and trolleybus system, among others, and soon after its formation it decided to replace the tram system mainly by trolleybuses, rather than undertake a heavy tramway renewal programme

A driver using a radio telephone in his cab to speak to the bus controller on duty

that would involve both vehicles and track. One advantage of the trolleybus over the tram was its greater flexibility which enabled it to draw up at the kerb to load and unload – most London streets were too narrow to allow passenger-loading islands alongside the tram track – and it did not need rails which were costly to install and maintain. By continuing to use electric vehicles, the Board was able to make use of the power stations and electric distribution system it had inherited. In 1935, therefore, London Transport started to convert the tramways to trolleybus operation, beginning with those parts of the system previously owned by the companies and smaller municipalities – mainly north of the River Thames – and leaving the largely conduit-type system formerly operated by the London County Council until last.

During the ten years from 1940 to 1950,

the London trolleybus network, for many years the largest in the world, was not greatly altered. The first major change came on 1 October 1950 when, under the first stage of London Transport's conversion programme, trolleybus route 612, from Battersea to Mitcham, was replaced by bus route 44, which also took over tram route 12 from London Bridge to Battersea and Wandsworth. The withdrawal of route 612 involved the complete abandonment of nearly 2 miles of trolleybus route between Battersea and Wandsworth and was the first reduction of the network.

After the war, London Transport decided that the traffic advantages already mentioned were such, and also because the trolleybus fleet and the electrical distribution system both required renewing, that it would rely entirely on oil-engined buses in the future.

In January 1959, two months before the conversion of trolleybuses to motor buses began, three services – routes 664, 683, and 695 – were withdrawn, other services in the areas concerned being adjusted.

The main conversion scheme started on 4 March 1959, and took place in 14 stages at roughly three-monthly intervals. The number of routes dealt with at each stage varied, but all involved about 100 trolleybuses. At the first stage, the two isolated routes in South-East London and the Sutton–Crystal Palace service were converted, and the next five stages saw the conversion of all routes operating east of the Lea Valley.

For stages 1, 2, and 3, 56-seat 'RT' type buses, made surplus elsewhere by falling passenger traffic, were used to replace the trolleybuses, making it possible to start the conversion earlier than would otherwise have been the case. For all subsequent stages new 64-seat 'RM' 'Routemaster' buses were used.

Stages 7 and 8, in the second half of 1960, were concerned with West London routes, operating north and south through Hammersmith and along the Uxbridge Road, and also the route up Highgate Hill. Under stages 9 to 12, electric street transport was removed from North London and the central area, leaving the north-west sector to be dealt with under stage 13 in January 1962 and, finally, at Stage 14, the oldest routes of all, in the south-west. The last trolleybuses made their last journeys on 8 May 1962.

The conversion programme had not only meant the acquisition of new vehicles and alterations to premises, but also the learning of new skills by the men who drove and maintained the fleet. For example, 2,851 trolleybus drivers had to be retrained to enable them to drive diesel buses.

There were 22 trolleybus depots in London, all but one – Bexleyheath – having been converted from tram depots at the appropriate time before the war. Acton depot was in use for about a year only, from April 1936, while conversion work was completed at Hanwell.

Wandsworth depot was the first to be converted to a bus garage, in October 1950 when route 612 was withdrawn. It had the distinction, shared with Highgate, now known as Holloway, of housing both trams and trolleybuses for 13 or so years.

Of the remaining 20 depots, five were closed as the conversion scheme proceeded; these were mainly small establishments housing between 30 and 50 vehicles and there were existing bus garages nearby.

The staff position continued to worsen in 1960, rising from a shortage of 8.5 per cent. at the beginning of the year to a peak of 15 per cent. in September. Proposals for a bonus scheme were rejected by the busmen but a straightforward wage increase in October improved the staff situation almost immediately so that services could be brought back to a reasonable level. One way in which the shortage of staff was eased was by re-scheduling services so that they could be run with the staff available.

In 1961 there appeared a 30ft.-long version of the 'RM' or 'Routemaster' bus. Because the 'RM' has no chassis it was a fairly simple matter to take the front and rear halves of a standard bus and insert a new centre section which would take four more passengers on each deck, bringing the seating capacity to 72 for a weight of only 7 tons 11 cwt. The original 'RM' buses could not have been built to that length because Ministry regulations at the time did not allow it – and there was a widespread feeling that a bus more than 27ft. 6in. long would not be suitable for London conditions. The first 30-ft. 'RM' buses, now lettered 'RML', entered service on route 104 and they proved so successful that after 1965 no more of the original length were built. A double-deck Green Line coach version of the 'RM' appeared in 1962, featuring air suspension at the rear and air-operated doors to the platform. It had 57 seats against the 64 of the standard 'RM' bus and was lettered 'RMC'. The 'RML' found its way into the Country as well as the Central bus fleet. In 1965 a lengthened version of the coach ('RCL') began running on the services eastward from Aldgate. It had 65 seats and was fitted with an 11.3-litre engine instead of the 9.6-litre engine of the 'RMC'. There was even a forward-entrance version of the 'RM' – the 'RMF' – which appeared at the Commercial Motor Show in 1962 but did not run in service in London.

In July 1961 an unpainted Routemaster bus was put into service on route 276 on weekdays and route 127 on Sundays to test durability, appearance, and public reaction. This followed the successful move to unpainted aluminium trains on the Underground which had been carried out without any violent public reaction. The unpainted bus (in fact certain parts which were moulded with the standard red colour as an integral part had to be painted to match the unpainted aluminium alloy) ran for some time and was nicknamed 'The Silver Lady', but the public liked its red buses and there were engineering disadvantages when it came to dealing with the minor knocks and scratches that buses running every day in heavy traffic must inevitably receive from time to time, and so the experiment was dropped.

In 1961 also, the long-lived 'RT' began at last, with the end of the trolleybus conversion, to be replaced by the 'RM'. Heaters began to be fitted to the Country bus fleet – a refinement by then expected by a travelling public used to heated private cars – and by 1963 all the Country buses had heaters and a start had been made on those of the Central area. A minor but happy thought was the loan, free, for a period of three hours, of pushchairs to people arriving at Hemel Hempstead bus station with small children to shop in the town. A similar scheme was started later at Harlow.

The year 1962 was the last for the London Transport Executive. Under the terms of the Transport Act 1962 nationalized transport was reorganized into a number of separate Boards corresponding more or less to the previous divisions of the British Transport Commission. On the last day of 1962 the London Transport Executive died, only to rise, Phoenix-like, the following morning as the London Transport Board with very similar membership but now directly responsible, once again, to the Minister of Transport. In its last year the Executive earned enough to pay its way, including its contribution to B.T.C. central charges.

Traffic conditions showed some improvement because of traffic measures (though in some cases these meant that buses could not take passengers where they wanted to go) and the staff position improved slightly. Because of these factors and an unusually large rise in population in the London Transport area – due mainly to Commonwealth citizens arriving before the Immigration Act controls came into force – the fall in traffic was not as marked as in previous years. Increasing car ownership and television viewing, however, continued to take their toll, and bad weather during the summer was no help, especially to the country services.

XV The Last Decade

AS far as the buses were concerned, the new London Transport Board began life on a muted note. The competition for labour in London was already at such a pitch that recruiting staff – suitable staff – was very difficult indeed. A fully-trained London bus driver finds no difficulty in obtaining a position as a commercial vehicle driver and many staff have been lost to this field in the past. It has to be acknowledged also that when there are plenty of five-day week jobs with regular hours offering – and the growth of unemployment in the last few years has had little impact on the London position – it needs a particular type of man to be willing to work on shifts, and at weekends, when his friends and family are at leisure. Also, a busman needs to live near his work so that he can get to the garage in the early morning or home again late at night. But suitable housing has become more and more difficult to find in London. In 1963 all this applied, and the search for staff was extended to north-east England and continued in Ireland and Barbados. A small team even visited Malta at the request of the Maltese Government and recruited a few staff there. The shortage of drivers reduced the need for conductors, but all conductors who expressed a wish to become drivers were given the opportunity and 426 qualified in 1963.

Despite this, to quote the annual report: 'In the previous two years the regularity and reliability of the bus services had been improving, but in 1963 the staff position deteriorated seriously and by the autumn the number of scheduled bus miles "lost" on Central Buses because crews were not available was over twice what it had been a year previously; a ban by bus staff on overtime and rest day working from the end of October doubled this percentage again. The mileage 'lost' because of traffic congestion also increased substantially in the same period. In

consequence, by the end of 1963, the standard of the bus services generally had fallen well below what the travelling public has been used to and is entitled to expect. There was naturally a substantial drop in the traffic carried on the road services. . . .

'As the end of the year approached it became clear from the trends of recruitment and wastage for bus operating staff, particularly drivers, that the position was unlikely to improve and that in the light of current and prospective demands for labour in the London area a solution would not be found by any improvement in wages and conditions of service within the framework of the Government's "guiding light" principle. Following discussions with the Ministries concerned, the Board concurred with the Government's proposal, announced on 20 November 1963, to appoint a special Committee of Inquiry under the chairmanship of Professor E. H. Phelps Brown to review and report on the pay and conditions of employment of the drivers and conductors of the Board's road services and related matters.'

The Committee issued an interim report on 16 December 1963, recommending interim rises in pay. These were agreed with the union and took effect from 18 December 1963. The ban on overtime and rest-day working was discontinued as part of the agreement and there was an immediate improvement in the frequency and regularity of the road services. But at the end of the year there was still a shortage of 1,840 drivers (12 per cent.) and 1,240 conductors (8 per cent.) in the Central bus fleet. In west London where the competition for labour was, and still is, especially strong, the shortage figures were often much higher at individual garages.

'The first essential', said the annual report, 'is to build up the strength of the bus operating staff, and the action to be taken in this direction must largely depend on the final findings of the Committee of Inquiry. The Board are firmly of the view that, if some increase in fares will enable them to pay the level of wages necessary to attract an adequate force of operating staff and so achieve a thoroughly reliable standard of service, the public would prefer such an increase to the present irregularity of running and the resulting excessive waits at bus stops'.

In many ways, what has just been said sets the keynote for the last ten years – a fight to maintain the bus services which Londoners need and expect in the face of constant staff shortages, rising costs, increasing street congestion, and an ever-growing population of cars – and a generation growing up to be car- rather than public transport-minded. Traffic congestion in particular took on a new complexion. While things became no worse in Central London, thanks to parking meters and other schemes of control, it was found that congestion was being pushed farther out from the centre. At points on the periphery of the central area delays in 1963 were the worst ever recorded until then. As the approaches were improved and the centre stabilized, the trouble was simply spreading farther out into what one of London Transport's officers was to call, aptly, the 'gluepot ring'.

The final report of the Phelps Brown committee opened the way to a new agreement with the busmen under which they received higher pay – including at last a bonus scheme – and better conditions. It was hoped that these factors would help to retain existing staff as well as recruit new. The agreement was not signed until June, and before that the staff position had weakened still more and congestion had reached such heights that the Board was moved to declare, 'Unless radical action is taken, the private car could in the foreseeable future stifle both the bus and itself'.

In case the reader should feel that these troubles were all avoidable, let it be said that London Transport was almost alone among all those responsible for transport in the great metropolitan cities of the world in having to make public transport self-supporting – instead of being municipally supported as a public service. It could not pay any rates it liked to its busmen because it had to maintain a commercial approach – not to **make** a profit, but at least to 'break even'. There were always Government guidelines on wages to be watched. And every other city in the more prosperous parts of the world was suffering the same problem of congestion. Some were also finding it hard to get staff.

As part of the agreement with the Transport & General Workers' Union after the Phelps Brown report, the union undertook to co-operate in measures to improve the service to the public and save vehicles and manpower. The measures included the use of more 72-seat 'RML' type buses, extension of one-man operation on the Country routes and its introduction on Central routes, and experiments with larger-capacity and 'standee' buses. Incidentally, the name 'standee', though of long and respectable parentage, was quickly dropped by London Transport, largely on the grounds that the buses had quite a number of seats, and the term 'multi-standing' was substituted in any announcements. As a result, orders were placed for nine high-capacity 46-seater single-deck buses, with front entrances and central exits, for one-man operation on country routes, 14 single-deck 49-seat luxury coaches for trials on express Green Line routes, 50 Atlantean and eight Fleetline double-deck front entrance buses in order to evaluate the operation of buses of this layout in London conditions, and six single-deck buses with seats for 25 and room for 50 to stand 'for experiments in handling big surges of rush-hour passengers in Central London, for example between main line termini and business centres. They will be fitted with coin-operated entrance barriers and separate exits'.

At last London Transport could begin to fight back. If it should be argued that the high-capacity 'multi-standing' buses men-

SMS type bus on Route 285 leaving the tunnel to the central airport area at Heathrow

tioned above for services to and from London termini sound very much like the recommendations of the Chambers report of 1955 the reply is simple – if not what might be expected. Until the latest agreement such a bus would have had to have a conductor. If a conductor were to be carried he might as well do his normal job. If he did, an 'RML' could be used which would give 72 *seats* as well as five standing and thus exceed the capacity of the new single-deckers as well as giving a much more comfortable, seated ride. Under the regulations, double-deckers could not be operated by one man. There was, of course, another factor. At the time of the Chambers report single-deck buses were limited to 30ft. in length and the number of standing passengers could not be more than half the number for whom seats were provided. This meant, in

practice, that a 'multi-standing' bus could not carry any more than the more comfortable double-decker. It was only when regulations permitted buses to be built with a length of 36ft. and a width of 8ft. 2½in. that the mathematics came out more or less right. Also, with earlier types of bus than the low-chassis ones then available from AEC, the entrance and exit steps would have been very much higher – and some people imagine them high even now, even though there is only a fractional difference between step heights on old and new vehicles. But more of the new buses later.

It was not until 1965 that the Government made positive moves towards recognizing London Transport's problems. Not much has been said about fares in this book because fares in themselves are not particularly interesting and vary as much with social conditions and the current demand for labour as with transport needs. It will have been obvious, however, between the lines that fares must have risen steadily as social conditions improved and London Transport's staff asked for higher pay partly to keep their place in the social scale, partly in accordance with the normal operation of the labour market, and partly in recognition of the larger vehicles they were called upon to manage. It is a far cry from the small horse bus to the 72-seat Routemaster and the even bigger buses of today. Higher pay, higher costs all round, and the inability to reduce expenses at the same rate as traffic fell – a garage needs much the same upkeep whether it is running 150 buses or 50 – had to be met from somewhere and higher fares, since London Transport, apart from a comparatively small amount from commercial advertising and management of its 'estates', has no other source of income, were unavoidable.

It was a proposal to increase fares yet again in 1965 which brought about Government intervention. The Minister of Transport said in the House of Commons that the Government had concluded that a thorough examination of the conditions under which the Board operated was necessary, including the possibility of even more extensive traffic management measures and also other measures of restraint of traffic. The Government were anxious that while this examination was being carried out the attractiveness of the Board's services should not be lessened and accordingly asked the Board to agree to postpone action for fares increases, at the same time giving an assurance that the Board would not have to bear the loss in revenue caused by this postponement.

As it happens, during the same year the Select Committee of the House of Commons on Nationalized Industries, which looks into the performance of one of the nationalized industries every year, was examining London Transport. Their report, issued in September, concluded that London Transport could perform its two main duties – about which the Board was becoming increasingly anxious – provided it had the right conditions in which to operate. The two statutory duties were to provide or secure the provision of an adequate and properly co-ordinated system of passenger transport for the Board's area, and to pay its way. As far as the buses were concerned, the conditions included giving them 'room to operate properly by according them some measure of priority as the greatest carriers of traffic, especially at peak hours, and by other steps taken to reduce congestion on the roads'. Also, London Transport, they said, needed the tools to do the job. In particular, on the roads it needed more buses that could be operated by one man. The Board needed also to carry still further the improvements in staff relations and staff productivity made possible by the Phelps Brown settlement.

When the Committee's Report was debated in the House of Commons on 9 December 1965, the Minister of Transport made a statement of Government policy, part of which stated: 'As a result of our analysis of the situation, we adopt the following broad objectives: first, to call a halt to the deterioration of London's transport facilities – of all kinds – and to make the positive improvements necessary to meet the economic and social needs of a great city, and to ensure that the traffic vital to those needs shall have freedom to move; secondly, to take measures to ensure the best use of scarce road space; thirdly, since we regard public transport systems as essential, to ensure that necessary public transport services are not only maintained but improved; fourthly, to find means to achieve a more equitable distribution of the burden of paying for London's transport in all its forms. To achieve these objectives, complementary measures will be needed, to discourage the use of private cars, notably at peak times, and to improve public transport.'

XVI The Last Decade—Rebirth

IN 1965, for the first time since 1958 – the year of the bus strike – London Transport failed to earn enough to meet in full the interest on its capital debt. There was a working surplus of £5.5 million, but interest charges were £6.5 million, swallowing up the surplus and leaving a deficit of £1 million. This was despite £3,850,000 from the Government in compensation for not raising fares, as explained in the last chapter. Although there was no increase in fares during the year, there was again a large drop in the number of bus and coach passengers – 5.3 per cent. Serious as this was, it was an improvement on the previous year when the fall was 7.3 per cent. The causes were the same as for so many years – more motor cars and more congestion and not enough staff. The trend towards congestion in the inner suburbs was again marked.

But now things began to change. London Transport officers had been looking at the operation of front-entrance double-deck buses in other parts of the country and had come to the conclusion that because the driver could help to look after the entrance and exit the conductor, not being tied to the platform at every stop, could collect fares more efficiently and there would be a better balance of work between the members of the crew. After Phelps Brown, the union had agreed to co-operate in various measures and the decision was taken to carry out comparative experiments using 50 Leyland Atlantean buses and 'RML' and 'RM' buses. Both the Atlanteans and 'RMLs' had 72 seats, but the Atlantean had double front-entrance doors operated by the driver. These buses were 30ft. 4in. long and 8ft. wide with 41 seats in the upper saloon and 31 in the lower, and were the first double-deckers with front entrances and doors to run in London. They had fully-automatic transmission, power steering, power handbrake, and weighed

8 tons 18 cwt. compared with the 7 tons 12 cwt. of the 72-seat 'RML'. The Atlanteans (or 'XA' type) and Routemasters were to run on routes where their use on existing frequencies would increase the seating capacity and also on routes on which the frequency would be reduced but, because of the greater seating capacity of the new buses, the number of seats offered would remain the same. These trials, it was hoped, would give information which could be used to determine the most suitable type of bus for London and especially for future replacements of the existing double-deckers.

The experiment began on Sunday, 7 November 1965 when the first 30 Atlanteans went into service on route 24 (Hampstead Heath–Charing Cross–Pimlico). The 'RMLs' had already begun running, from November 1, on route 76 (Lower Edmonton–Bank–Victoria). The other routes concerned in the initial stages of the experiment were 67 (Northumberland Park–London Docks) using the 72-seat Routemasters and 271 (Highgate Village–Moorgate) using the Atlanteans.

One-man operation in the Central (red) bus area of London had started nearly a year before when on Wednesday, 18 November 1964 four outer suburban routes began running with the driver in sole charge. The routes were: 201 Hampton Court Station–Kingston (operated by Norbiton garage); 206 Hampton Court Station–Claygate (operated by Fulwell garage); 216 Kingston–Staines (operated by Kingston garage); and 250 Hornchurch Garage–Epping Town (operated by Romford (North Street) garage).

The 24 single-deck 'RF' 39-seater buses involved in working these four routes were converted from ordinary single-deckers by fitting to the entrance power-operated doors, controlled by the driver/conductor. Passengers paid their fares as they boarded and the

London's first Bus Lane – at Park Lane

whether a bus with seven more seats than the familiar 'RF' could be successfully operated by one man on wide-headway routes, and also whether some routes too busy for the standard single-deck buses but with insufficient traffic to fill double-deck vehicles could be successfully operated with the new 46-seat buses. Only one of these buses actually ran in the country area, the others being converted for Red Arrow services before going into use.

The eight Daimler Fleetlines with bodies by Park Royal Vehicles Ltd. for the country area were of special interest. The bodies were very similar to those of the Central area Atlanteans and also had 72 seats, 41 in the upper saloon and 31 in the lower: the front entrance had folding doors under the control of the driver. These buses were 30ft. 6in. long and 8ft. wide and had Gardner 6LX vertical direct-injection engines mounted at the rear. Fully automatic transmission was fitted and suspension, as on the Atlantean, was by leaf springs. They were known as the 'XF' series and weighed 8 tons 18 cwt.

The unusual feature of these buses was that it was possible to close a door over the staircase entrance after the morning peak was over and to work the bus as a one-man vehicle, using the lower saloon only, until the evening peak. Then the door could be opened and a conductor could board the bus again until the end of the peak. It was also possible to run the buses with the top deck shut off at weekends when traffic is light. When the buses were ordered, that type of operation was not allowed by Ministry regulations, but no difficulty was then expected in obtaining permission since the Ministry had let it be known that regulations would not be allowed to stand in the way of design progress. As the regulations stood, a double-deck bus had to have a conductor. It made no difference that a closed door prevented the upper deck from being used.

The Fleetlines went to East Grinstead garage in the first instance and worked on route 424 (Reigate–East Grinstead).

The regulations were amended in 1966 to

driver/conductor gave change and issued tickets from a machine attached to a counter on the nearside door of his cab. The four routes selected as the first batch for conversion had been running at a considerable loss and might otherwise have had to be reduced or even withdrawn. As it happens, two of them had been one-man operated before the war – when there were 11 one-man operated routes. They were routes 206 and 216, both of which had been operated with the small Dennis Dart vehicles.

As already mentioned, for experimental operation in the country area, London Transport ordered nine one-man operated single-deck 46-seater buses with front entrance and centre exit fitted with power-operated doors under the control of the driver. These buses, 36ft. long and 8ft. 2½in. wide, had Strachans (Coachbuilders) Ltd. bodies and AEC Merlin chassis. They were known as the 'XMBs', and with them it was possible to find out

*Early post-war experiments with automatic fare collection on London's buses.
The Country bus route 430 was one of those selected for trials*

*Passengers read their fare from a faretable
carried over the machine*

allow the 'XF' buses to be worked in the way intended, but the need to provide a conductor at peak periods made this system of working financially doubtful, and the experiment was discontinued in 1967 when the regulations were again amended to permit double-deck operation with one man on approved routes.

There were also six experimental single-deck multi-standing buses with bodies by Strachans (Coachbuilders) Ltd. on AEC Merlin chassis. They were 36ft. long and 8ft. 2½in. wide and carried 73 passengers, 25 in seats at the rear of the bus and 48 standing. The front entrance and centre exit were both fitted with power-operated doors under

[117]

the control of the driver. Passengers entering the bus passed through twin tripod-type gates each operated by a single coin, a 6d., which released the gate so that a passenger could move through into the main body of the bus. The buses began to run on Monday, 18 April 1966 on a route between Victoria and Marble Arch via Grosvenor Place and Park Lane. The route was given the number 500. Passengers were carried in the peak travel direction only, i.e. from Victoria in the morning and to Victoria in the evening, the buses returning as quickly as possible empty. Consideration had been given from the start to the possible use of the vehicles in the off-peaks on a circular route between a station and the West End shopping area and the route chosen was between Victoria and Oxford Street. The route chosen for the peak services was relatively free from traffic congestion, largely because of the Hyde Park Corner and Park Lane one-way schemes, and it was hoped that it would be possible to offer a faster service than was given by the ordinary buses.

The multi-standing buses were given the name 'Red Arrow' and weighed, unladen, 7 tons 14 cwt. They were fitted with an AEC AH 691 horizontal direct-injection engine, mounted at the rear, giving, when derated to London Transport requirements, 147 b.h.p. at 1,800 r.p.m., and automatic transmission. Suspension was by a combination of air and leaf springing. They were known as 'XMS' buses; experiments were carried out on them with a change-giving machine, but troubles were experienced with bent and worn coins.

Another feature of the Red Arrows was, and is, that the driver has a public address system with which he can announce the names of stops.

An example of the complexity of arranging this type of service was that, because the flat fare was not based on distance, London Transport had to make a special application to the Transport Tribunal to be allowed to charge it as a 'reasonable' fare.

All these experiments were designed to show up the advantages and disadvantages of each type of vehicle and method of working before final decisions were made on the type of bus to be ordered in quantity to replace existing buses – particularly the 'RT'. However, the staff shortage was such that it had been essential to take advantage as soon as possible of the new freedom to use one-man operated (o.m.o.) buses in order to restore a more frequent bus service to sadly-depleted routes and to others which, uneconomic to run with double-deckers, might be made to pay – or at least to lose less – with one-man buses. The advent, under the new regulations, of the 36-ft. long bus with its greater number of seats did something to replace the seating capacity of the double-deck 'RT'. With this in mind the Board ordered 150 single-deck 36-ft. long buses in mid-1965.

There was no time for the Board to design its own buses – the need was too urgent. As it was, the new buses could not be available until 1967. They were to be on 'Merlin' chassis again, like the first Red Arrows, but would have Metropolitan-Cammell-Weymann bodies with various layouts. Fifty-two buses were to have 50 seats and a front entrance/exit for use on Central bus routes in the suburban areas; 33 would be Country buses with 45 seats, a front entrance, and a central exit; 16 would have 25 seats and space for 48 standing passengers for an extension of the Red Arrow services; and 49 vehicles with a similar layout to the Red Arrows were to be used for experimental flat-fare suburban routes.

To tackle traffic congestion, at the request of the Minister of Transport a working party of representatives of the Greater London Council, the Metropolitan Police, and London Transport was set up under the chairmanship of the Council's Director of Highways & Transportation to see how management could help bus services. The working party concentrated its attention on action which could be taken in the short term, particularly in the period up to the end of 1966. This included 16 more urban clearways and many more new controlled parking zones and new major one-way schemes. London Transport, although pressing for quicker action than the Police and G.L.C. thought feasible, realized that there were limitations on what could be done.

The working party estimated that the net result, up to the end of 1966, of all the traffic management measures it had discussed and found feasible would be the prevention of further deterioration of bus services, or at best some marginal improvement. Similar measures in the future were likely to be similar in effect because traffic was continuously rising. The working party pointed out that this might seem a disappointing outcome from a very substantial traffic management programme but without the programme there would be a very serious deterioration in bus services. If any radical improvement in road conditions for buses were to be achieved, it could only come by restricting the volume of other traffic using bus routes at busy times.

In 1966 itself there were major developments at Government level, beginning on February 24 with an announcement by the Minister of Transport that a Transport Co-ordinating Council for London was to be set up with representatives of the Minister, the G.L.C., London Transport, British Railways, the London boroughs, and the Trades Union Congress all working together 'to plan a concerted attack on the problems of public transport in London'. When the new Council met on 3 March 1966 it decided to establish five groups to deal with various aspects of its task. Group I was to deal with transport operations and traffic management co-ordination, Group II with interchanges, Group III with public transport investment, Group IV with highways planning, and Group V with freight transport. London Transport representatives sat regularly on Groups I–III and as required on the other two groups.

The Government also accepted that London Transport could no longer reconcile the two main duties laid upon it – to provide an adequate service *and* pay its way. It was agreed that the provision of services should be supported from public funds while a fundamental re-appraisal of the role of public transport in London was carried out. The Transport Finances Act, 1966 gave powers for grants up to £16 million to meet revenue deficits expected up to the end of 1968.

The Government and the Board also agreed to undertake a joint review of the Board's financial needs and commercial policies and of the main operating and management problems arising from them. The Review was carried out under the control of a Directing Group chaired by the late Stephen Swingler, then Joint Parliamentary Secretary to the Minister of Transport, with representatives of the Ministry and the Board, together with two distinguished industrialists and a working London Transport bus driver.

On transport in the country as a whole the Minister published a White Paper on Transport Policy in July 1966, which emphasized the need for land use and transport to be planned together and envisaged that single authorities would need to be established for major conurbations with responsibility for highways, traffic, and public transport suitably linked with land use planning. The Minister proposed to take powers to create conurbation transport authorities under broad local authority control, or suitably linked with local authorities, whose duty would be to integrate public transport in urban regions. The White Paper accepted that public transport could not play an effective part without financial help. It expressed the view that, where financial assistance was needed, those who benefited from the existence of the service should contribute to its cost and that the first source of 'outside' support should be the local community. However, the Government proposed to take powers to provide financial help for the construction or major improvement of public transport structures that formed part of comprehensive local transport plans – railways, new forms of reserved track transport

A 'split-entrance' single-deck bus running on a Central bus route in the late 1960s

Entrance to a double-deck bus, converted for one man operation. Note the box with its transparent top for collecting the fares

which might be developed, and terminal and interchange facilities used by public transport. A large and centrally co-ordinated programme of research and development was to include the setting up of a group, on which London Transport was to be represented, to examine the technical and operational problems of one-man bus operation.

The proposal to establish a single authority for each major conurbation area was to include London, though the Government pointed out that London's transport problems were unique in

[120]

size and complexity. Meanwhile London Transport had been looking at some large cities abroad and was impressed with the progress made with the constitution of authorities with responsibilities over the whole transport field. The Board thought, and said, that the division of responsibilities in the London area was not effective in securing conditions in which transport movements of all kind could be carried on. 'Major town-planning decisions', it declared, 'are taken by authorities which are not directly concerned in the planning or provision of transport except so far as they are responsible for highway construction; they are providers neither of railway facilities nor of the passenger services which will be required on the highways, and planning is deficient in this respect. Further, the present organization fails to secure a just balance between the interest of private and public passenger transport on the roads in relation to the needs of the whole community'.

Clearly the stage was being set for a major upheaval. Passenger traffic was still dropping on the buses and coaches, and a fares revision in January 1966 and a Central busmen's ban on overtime and rest-day working between 23 January and 26 February 1966 which led to the temporary withdrawal of 40 routes had not helped. Although reductions in services were made following this fall in traffic, there was still a shortage of bus crews amounting to 12 per cent. at the beginning of the year and in consequence some 9 per cent. of the scheduled bus mileage could not be worked. A wage increase in June helped to improve the position later in the year. New schedules were introduced to match services more closely to the availability of staff and local rationalization schemes were introduced. One-man operation was extended and by the end of 1966 only four single-deck buses in the Country area were still crew-operated. On 10 July 1966 the first o.m.o. Green Line route – a High Wycombe–Romford service via Amersham, Watford, St. Albans, Hertford, and Harlow – began operations. Many

of the 'RF' coaches – in good condition mechanically – were modernized during the year to fit them for a further period of service.

Changes in the system of bus maintenance were introduced at the works and in the garages. Experience of the 'RM' bus made a substantial increase in the period which could be worked between major overhauls possible as long as some additional work was undertaken in the garages. This reduced the work at Aldenham and made a saving of about 450 staff. As a result a new works layout was planned for Aldenham, and when completed this allowed some 250,000 sq. ft. of covered space to be leased, bringing in a substantial rent.

A new management organization was brought into being in 1966 for the Central bus fleet after study by management consultants. The main effect was to give more freedom and responsibility to local managers.

Perhaps the most important event of 1966 from the passenger's point of view, however, was a glimpse of the future in 'Reshaping London's Bus Services', a report published by London Transport in September. The report told the public of its four-point plan for reshaping bus services to combat traffic congestion and staff shortage – the most severe problems affecting bus services. It explained the background of the continuous fall for 15 years in the number of bus passengers carried – especially at weekends – and pointed out that this trend was likely to continue as the ownership and use of private cars increased. As peak service requirements (the peaks were becoming more concentrated and the proportion of total traffic carried in them was rising as off-peak traffic fell) dictated the numbers of buses and staff needed, the increasing disparity between peak and off-peak demand made the whole operation less and less economical. The report also repeated and emphasized the difficulties caused by congestion, its unpredictability, and the problems of countering its effects. Delays and bunching of buses caused by road congestion, it pointed out, often react until well after the

*'MBA' type bus on Red Arrow Route 505
passing the National Gallery*

forward to improving productivity was one-man operation. The Board believed that this method of operation, already extensively employed on single-deck buses, must be applied throughout the bus system as quickly as possible. But there could be no sudden, dramatic change; new fare collection equipment and new vehicles were required, the pattern of routes would have to be altered, and there must be no undue hardship imposed on the staff.

The plan proposed had four points : (i) routes must be shortened; (ii) one-man operation must be extended throughout the fleet; (iii) more standing accommodation must be provided on short routes; and (iv) new methods of fare collection must be devised. To achieve these objectives it was proposed that the principal trunk routes with heavy passenger loads between the centre and the suburbs would continue to be worked by large double-deck buses with conductors. Many routes would be shortened to counter the effects of traffic congestion and so that control over their running could be exercised more effectively. Within the centre of London (West End and City) single-deck buses like the existing Red Arrows, worked by one man and with a flat fare, would provide limited-stop services between points where there were large and regular movements. In the peaks, these routes would be largely based on main-line railway stations; outside the peaks, they would be designed principally to serve shoppers and visitors.

peak hour traffic itself has ended, and spread to districts well away from the congestion which caused the trouble.

The shortage of manpower, the report declared, could only be overcome by reducing the number of staff required; in other words, by increasing productivity. Little more could be done to increase the effective capacity of the two-man double-decker, and the way

In the suburbs, local routes would be based on the main business and shopping centres

[122]

and would also serve as feeders to trunk routes and Underground or British Railways stations. They would be worked by single-deck buses, with one-man operation, and would have a flat fare. They would be much shorter than most existing suburban routes. As not all suburban journeys could be covered satisfactorily by flat-fare routes, some suburban buses would operate on longer routes with graduated fares; they would be worked by one-man single-deck buses but for the time being, double-deck operation with two men would remain on the principal suburban routes. The Country bus route pattern generally would not be altered, but one-man working would be much extended, while Green Line coaches would continue to provide an express service, probably developed with new cross-connections. The coaches would be one-man operated.

Flat fares could be collected by machine, but sophisticated equipment able to collect graduated fares and ensure that passengers paid the correct fare for the journey had to be developed. The equipment had to be easy to operate, reliable, and work fast enough to prevent excessive delays at stops.

This, then, was the blue-print for the years ahead. It was clear that the price for reducing the effects of congestion would be that some passengers would have to change buses more often because of the shorter routes – although in any case nearly four out of five journeys are for two miles or less. Changing buses could in some cases entail higher fares because the two separate sections might cost more than a through journey, but here again the numbers affected would be comparatively low. Flat fares, as with the Red Arrows, could cost some people more compared with an ortho-dox graduated fare journey, since the fare had to be pitched at an economic level. With the first 'Red Arrows', the throughout Victoria–Marble Arch journey became cheaper but to intermediate points it cost more – but the alternative of the ordinary services remained in being.

Although there had not been time to design its own single-deck 36ft.-long O.M.O. buses (another 375 of which were ordered at the end of 1966), London Transport's design team had not been idle. Since 1964, with AEC and Park Royal, it had been working on a front entrance, rear-engined, version of the versatile Routemaster bus. It appeared late in 1966 and was the first rear-engined double-deck bus of integral construction to be built in Britain. The 'FRM' (Front entrance

'FRM' type bus crossing Westminster Bridge, with the Houses of Parliament in the background

Routemaster) was 31ft. 3in. long and 8ft. wide, with 31 seats on the lower deck and 41 'on top'. Although of completely different layout, it incorporated some 60 per cent. of standard Routemaster parts.

Features of the 'FRM' included electrically-operated folding doors with centre pillar; independent front suspension using coil springs, and air suspension at the rear; automatic transmission; power-assisted steering; twin-circuit hydraulic brakes; fluorescent lighting; a thermostatically-controlled, fan-operated combined ventilating and heating system obviating opening windows; vertical AEC AV691 11.3-litre engine giving 150 b.h.p. at 1,800 r.p.m. transversely mounted on the nearside at the rear of the body, with gearbox on the offside; and a weight of only $8\frac{1}{2}$ tons.

It has been tested to compare its engineering performance with that of the standard 30ft. rear-entrance Routemaster ('RML') and other experimental 72 seat 30ft. vehicles – Atlantean ('XA') and Fleetline ('XF') buses on Leyland and Daimler chassis respectively and more recently has been working as a one-man-operated bus in south London. It is still considered by many to have been the finest double-deck bus ever built in Britain.

Unfortunately, the 'FRM' was heavier than the 30-ft. 'RML', though weight reductions could have been made, but in the quantities required by London Transport it was estimated that it would have been considerably more expensive. At the time it was produced one-man operation of double-deck buses was neither allowed nor even in sight. The front-entrance layout did not therefore have the value it was to assume the following year. When the 'FRM' appeared the drive was for high-capacity O.M.O. single-deckers, another 450 of which were ordered in 1967. The 'FRM' has, however, continued in service and has proved itself a reliable design.

Because of the five-day week introduced for bus crews, there was a general revision of schedules on all London Transport road ser-vices on 31 December 1966. The general effect was to widen the intervals between buses or coaches but to make them more reliable. Recruitment improved and wastage was reduced in the early part of 1967 as a result of the improved conditions and increased wages paid in two stages – December 1966 and July 1967 – following the end of the Government-imposed standstill on wages which had been recommended by the Prices and Incomes Board.

These factors enabled the mileage scheduled to be much more nearly approached than in the previous year, with only 2.4 per cent. 'lost' instead of 8.4 per cent. Also, about 100 extra buses could be operated in the Central area. The improvements led to an increase of 7 million passenger journeys during the year and considerably less time spent by passengers in queueing, but the better services cost London Transport more than it gained in extra revenue.

The main news of 1967 did not come until December 15, when the Minister of Transport and the Leader of the Greater London Council jointly announced that the G.L.C. was to become the statutory transport planning authority for London with wide responsibilities and powers for major highway functions, traffic, and public passenger transport services. The Council would appoint the Members of a London Transport Executive to be established under the new powers and would have effective control over policies, finance, and the broad lines of operations without being involved in the day-to-day management of the Underground network and bus services in the Greater London area, for which the Executive would be responsible. The Minister would put London Transport on a sound financial footing before the take-over and the financial arrangements would include a major write-off of the capital debt of the London Transport Board. The G.L.C. would obtain wider highway and traffic powers so that it could have unified direction of policy and planning. Procedural reforms would be introduced so that executive action and enforcement in these fields could be quicker and more effective. The future of London Transport bus and coach services outside the G.L.C. boundary was left for further discussion.

The British Rail commuter services would not come directly under the Council's control in the same way as London Transport services, but British Railways fares would be subject to consultation with the Council. The G.L.C.'s transport planning powers would enable it to bring these services into a common plan.

It was also announced, in the Transport Bill placed before Parliament in December 1967, that the Government would take powers to make grants, normally at 75 per cent. of the approved cost, towards major transport projects, including bus stations, depots, and interchange facilities and the provision of new rail and bus systems. There was also a grant scheme for approved types of new buses under which, from the autumn of 1968, the Government would pay 25 per cent. of the cost. An additional fuel grant was also proposed to set off fuel duty, increasing the grant to 19d. a gallon and saving London Transport over £1 million a year.

The Joint Review of London Transport's financial needs and policies controlled by the Directing Group under the chairmanship of Stephen Swingler, begun in 1966, was completed in 1968 and in January the Group made its report. (It was published as part of a White Paper under the title 'Transport in London' the following July.) In its comments on the report, the White Paper said:

'Judged against transport undertakings in large cities abroad which provide a similarly comprehensive range of services, London Transport have done well. They have so far had no capital grants for investment expenditure. Fares, though often criticized, are lower than in many foreign undertakings. They have gone up less, compared with prewar, than prices in many industries which do not face the same combination of adverse circumstances: a labour-intensive service industry

hit by falling demand and by a rapidly worsening operating environment.'

Various recommendations in the White Paper were embodied in the Transport (London) Bill introduced into Parliament in November 1968.

Against the background of all this administrative activity, services on the ground began to change. A productivity agreement with the Transport & General Workers' Union in July 1968 made it possible at last to bring the new long single-deck buses into operation. Deliveries had already begun but until this agreement had been reached the buses had had perforce to be stored in the works and garages. Reference has been made earlier to the various layouts involved but there was an additional design to cater for a simplified fare scale (known as 'coarsened fares') in which both entry streams from the twin front entrance were equipped for automatic ticket issue. These had seats for 25 and standing room for 41.

All the first orders were for 36-ft. buses, but it became evident that their length would be unacceptable on some routes and their movement and storage in some garages would cause difficulties, the capacity of some garages being seriously reduced. It was found possible, by a revision of the layout of the seating and the fare collection equipment, to get almost the same capacity in a bus 33ft. 5in. long and from autumn 1969 all deliveries were of this length. Also, daily experience with the suburban flat-fare buses made it evident that more seats, even though it entailed reducing the total capacity, would be more popular with passengers and have an overall advantage, so seven seats were added in the standing area in the front part of these buses, which have the main seating at a higher level to the rear of the centre exit.

The reshaping plan came to life, after the initial schemes had been made and remade as the stock of new buses grew but could not be put into service, on 7 September 1968, when what was probably the largest single revision of services ever made in London in one day was carried out. It entailed alterations affecting some 1,100 buses – about a fifth of the London fleet – and the introduction of 177 O.M.O. buses of the Red Arrow, conventional O.M.O., or the new suburban flat-fare types.

The main changes included seven new Red Arrow routes: 501 (Waterloo–Aldgate via the Strand underpass); 502 (Waterloo–Liverpool Street); 503 (Waterloo–Victoria via Westminster Bridge); 504 (Waterloo–Liverpool Street); 505 (Marylebone–Aldwych in peak hours: Waterloo–Portman Square in off-peak hours); 506 (Victoria–Piccadilly Circus); and 507 (Waterloo–Victoria via

station was opened with direct access to the railway station – served by the Eastern Region Chingford–Liverpool Street line as well as the Victoria Line, which at that stage ran only to Highbury & Islington.

Another scheme which was implemented on the same day was centred on the Wood Green area where London Transport has a bus garage almost opposite Wood Green Piccadilly Line station and, at the other end of the High Road shopping area, a large area – now converted to a covered bus station – next to Turnpike Lane Station, also on the Piccadilly Line. Both shops and stations

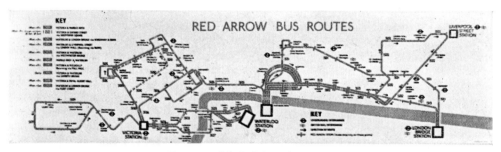

Route map of the Red Arrow bus services

Lambeth Bridge). All these were Monday-Friday routes except 504, which was a Saturday variation of 502. The somewhat strange-looking pattern of 505, which served Charing Cross Station, was due to the need to provide reliefs for the drivers – a difficult matter for routes running entirely within the West End where there are few suitable facilities. In general, one bus on conventional routes serving the same streets was withdrawn for every two Red Arrows put into service, so that overall the service was improved.

At Walthamstow three O.M.O. routes of the conventional type and one new flat-fare route were introduced in forming feeder routes to Walthamstow Central Station, served by the new Victoria Line from September 1. The whole pattern of routes in the area was changed in an upheaval affecting 400 buses and involving seven new routes and changes to 19 others. At the same time a new bus

already attracted a great deal of short distance traffic and the garage and bus station were ideal places in which buses used on the short feeder bus routes envisaged could turn and stand. Forty new flat-fare buses were used and 300 double-deck buses operating on 16 routes over 180 miles of route were affected in changes which shortened and rationalized some of the longer trunk routes and created a system which gave scope for eventual conversion of many routes to one-man operation.

Other conversion schemes followed, notably 'flat-fare' schemes in the Rotherhithe and Surrey Docks area in October and in the Ealing area in November. In the Country area five 'Autofare' O.M.O. buses – in which passengers bought tickets from a machine – were introduced as well as eight 36-ft. conventional O.M.O. buses with 45 seats replacing lower-capacity 'RF' buses.

Red Arrow bus on Route 503 in Parliament Square

The great changes of 1968 were marred by several things, the main one being the shortage of drivers. Although conductors made surplus by the o.m.o. conversions – if not already transferred elsewhere to fill vacancies – were, where possible, trained as drivers, there was a net loss of more than 1,000 drivers during the year and at the end of December there was a 12 per cent. shortage of both drivers and conductors. The next year

The Bus Station at Walthamstow provides bus/rail interchange with the Victoria Line and British Rail (Eastern Region) trains

the position grew worse and by September 1969 there was a 19 per cent. shortage of drivers and an 18 per cent. shortage of conductors. In parts of west and north-west London it was up to 30 per cent. The number of passengers travelling by Green Line continued to fall and services, as usual following and not anticipating the fall in traffic, had to be reduced despite many conversions to one-man operation. In all, the scheduled mileage of Green Line routes was reduced by 18 per cent.

London Transport learned a lot of lessons in the first months of operating the new buses. Complaints had been expected about falling standards from those who did not understand the situation in which London Transport found itself or who were resistant to change – as most of us are! The familiar double-deck 'RT' which had been running for so many years, with its normally helpful and cheerful conductor ready to hand the pushchair in and out or assist elderly people to their seats, was swept away and replaced by a long monster which often could not get into the kerb because of parked cars and was therefore more difficult to enter; in which a long open area had to be crossed, clutching handrails, and a step negotiated, before one could get a seat; which even the most active could not board – illicitly and dangerously but time-savingly – when held up in traffic or at lights because doors were now fitted – and those doors were at the 'wrong' end of the bus. And to cap it all London Transport changed the routes and even the route numbers from the ones that had been on the tip of the tongue for so long.

Readers will have gathered why all this was done. In some cases matters were so serious that it was 'One-man buses or no buses at all', but it was a great shock to many people. The passengers who took it all in their stride were the commuters who used the Red Arrows. They were used to standing in trains and used to buying tickets from machines. They did not mind a few more minutes standing in a moving bus if it saved their standing in a queue. They popped their coins into the Red Arrow twin gates and boarded at high speed. Even the failure of the original machines to stand up to intensive use in a moving bus did not worry them – they just accepted the new ones and they almost always have the right change ready in their hands.

In the suburbs the story was different, especially in the off-peak when elderly people, women burdened with shopping baskets or children or both, and people who travelled only occasionally, were concerned. Despite advertisements, newspaper reports, posters, buses placed on display locally in advance with inspectors to show how everything worked, and pamphlets through every door in the area affected, people did not know what to do when faced with the new buses for the first time. The consequence was that they took longer to board, the bus got behind schedule – some a long way behind because they had many passengers and some not at all because they had only a few – and the services became irregular – two together or a long gap with no bus at all. This meant that a service designed to have enough seats for all off-peak passengers was so unevenly loaded that standing was sometimes needed even in the off-peak.

The long storage time during the rather wet summer of 1968 waiting the outcome of negotiations gave rise to corrosion problems and created difficulties with the mechanism of the buses. Many went out of service for a short period with door troubles or troubles with the fare-collection machines.

Gradually most of these troubles were overcome – though some are still there. Passengers began to get used to the buses and more and more had their money ready as they boarded. Some of the fare collection ideas or machines have been scrapped and others have been tried – they are too numerous to detail here – and the complaints have become fewer as London Transport has arranged schedules to give more boarding time and fitted extra seats, as already described, into the standing area of suburban buses.

Changes in the regulations allowed double-deck buses to be operated by one man from 1967 (on approved routes) and the experimental Atlanteans were converted for this purpose, the first being introduced on route 233 between Croydon and the Roundshaw Estate in November 1969.

One of the most successful variations of the many fare-collecting methods has been the 'split-entrance' bus in which passengers who know the fare and have the right money enter on the right-hand side of the entrance, buy their ticket from a machine and pass into the bus through a turnstile. Other passengers enter on the left-hand side and buy their tickets from the driver.

This type of collection was adopted for the first purpose-built O.M.O. double-deck buses ordered by London Transport to come into service in 1970 (of which more later).

In 1969 the orders for 650 single-deck 36-ft. buses were completed and the first few of 100 of the 33ft. 5in. buses were delivered. Orders were placed for another 300 of these shorter buses with the split-entrance layout and another 100 of the purpose-built O.M.O. double-deckers already mentioned, of which 17 were already on the way, were ordered. In yet another fare-collection variation, the converted Atlantean O.M.O. double-deckers for flat-fare routes were fitted with a collection box similar to those widely used in the U.S.A. The passenger drops his fare into a transparent box where both he and the driver can see it. When the driver has satisfied himself that it is the correct money he presses a lever and the money drops into a locked compartment which cannot be opened until the bus goes back to the garage. No tickets are used with this system.

This is perhaps a suitable place for a word about bus control mentioned earlier in connection with the B.E.S.I. system introduced in 1957 and afterwards extended. To improve supervision on the road and enable experienced inspectors to get to the scene of any

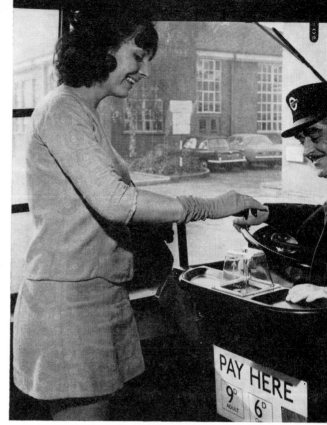

One of the first modern fare boxes to be brought into use in London. The passenger drops her exact fare in the box under the eye of the driver. When he is satisfied that it is the proper amount, he operates a control which allows the coins to drop into a locked container which can only be opened at the garage

difficulty in quick time, radio-fitted cars were introduced during the 1960s and proved so successful that the system was extended with cars available in all sections of London. There have also been small-scale experiments with inspectors carrying 'walkie-talkie' radios and, after a limited trial in 1968, a large-scale experiment was carried out with radios fitted to buses on route 74. This is being extended to 236 buses on the seven routes already controlled by the B.E.S.I. system.

Driver to controller radios are also being fitted to 18 buses on route 76 to assess the value of the radio link without the 'B.E.S.I.' control system. If these experiments prove

Marconi bus control system. Prototype installation in bus controller's office, 1973

The 'Silexine Paint' bus; the first bus painted completely with a colour scheme of a manufacturer under a long-term advertising contract with London Transport Commercial Advertising

successful it is expected that radio links may be extended to most routes, together with other control systems on the most heavily congested routes.

A bus location and control system, which with the aid of a computer calculates and records centrally the exact location of each bus on a route by measuring the wheel revolutions, is being tested on buses on route 11 in the near future and should be in full operation on this route during 1973.

Additional radio-fitted cars have been added to the bus mobile-supervision fleet, and centralized control of these cars has been established to co-ordinate their activities. Other control methods are now being tried. The main object is to counteract the effects of 'bunching' (mostly caused through traffic congestion) and to get services running regularly again as soon as possible.

At the end of 1969, under the terms of the Transport (London) Act 1969, the London Transport Board ceased to be and was replaced on 1 January 1970 by the London Transport Executive, responsible no longer direct to the Government but to the Greater London Council. All the Members of the Board were appointed Members of the Executive except Sir Maurice Holmes, the Chairman, who had stated that he did not wish to be considered for appointment. The new Chairman appointed was Sir Richard Way.

The last day of 1969 was also the last on which London Transport was responsible for the Country and Green Line services which had risen so dramatically after the war only to suffer, later, the effects of the tremendous boom in car ownership. They were vested in London Country Bus Services Ltd., a newly-formed subsidiary of the National Bus Company.

XVII Today and Tomorrow

WHEN the new London Transport Executive came into being on 1 January 1970 it found itself responsible for the management and day-to-day operation of services in a much smaller area – about 630 sq. miles mostly contained within a radius of about 15 miles from Charing Cross and following more or less the Greater London boundaries. Although this looks so much smaller than the previous 2,000 or so sq. miles, the real difference is much less since London Transport retained all the Underground railways inside or outside the area (though they are not part of this story) and lost only the comparatively small Country and Green Line fleet. The bulk of the bus fleet – the red buses, some of which run outside the G.L.C. boundary – were still in London Transport's care.

London Transport continued to be a public authority in its own right under the terms of the Transport (London) Act 1969 but the Greater London Council was established as the transportation authority for Greater London and was given overall policy and financial control of London Transport. The main duty of London Transport is to conduct its affairs on a commercial basis and in such a way as to meet the financial and operating objectives set for it by the G.L.C.

Subject to this, as the first report of the new Executive put it, the Act lays down the Executive's general duty as being 'to exercise and perform its functions, in accordance with principles from time to time laid down or approved by the Council, in such manner as, in conjunction with the Railways Board and the National Bus Company, and with due regard to efficiency, economy, and safety of operation, to provide or secure the provision of such public passenger transport services as best meets the needs for the time being of Greater London. . . .

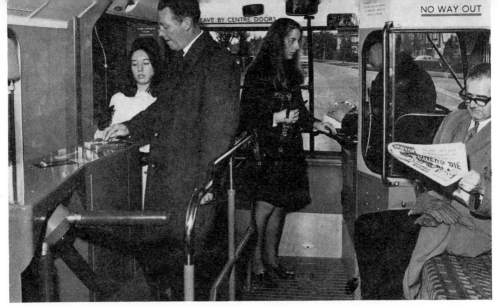

The 'split-entry' system on a 'DMS' bus. One passenger pays the driver while two, more in the other stream, buy their tickets from the machine

'In addition to the power of the Council to give directions to the Executive in relation to specific matters referred to in the Act, the Council may give to the Executive general directions as to the exercise and performance of its functions in relation to matters appearing to the Council to affect the policies and measures which it is the duty of the Council under the Act to develop, organize, or carry out.'

By the end of 1969 there were 517 single-deck one-man operated buses working on Monday to Friday services, including 55 Red Arrows, and it had been shown that double-deck buses could be successfully operated by one man. The new Executive decided to continue the policies of the former Board in this direction with the emphasis for new buses on double-deckers with a much higher proportion of seats than the single-deckers, thus giving much more passenger comfort.

Apart from two new 'Red Arrow' routes, most 1970 changes were in south-west London. By the end of 1970, 788 single-deck and 35 double-deck one-man buses were in use on 95 routes. All but 38 of the new buses delivered in that year were of the one-man operated 'split-entrance' type. The 38 were designed for conventional O.M.O. with passengers paying the driver.

The transparent fare-box system used on the Atlantean double-deck O.M.O. buses, described in the last chapter, was also applied in 1970 to the 194 single-deck buses on suburban flat-fare routes, doing away with the coin-operated tripod gates fitted previously. This was part of the drive to simplify and speed up fare collection systems so that passengers could board more quickly and the bus could spend less time at stops. This is important not only because slow boarding cuts down the overall speed with which the bus covers its route, so that individual passenger's journeys take longer, but because a bus moving faster can do more work and cover the route more times in a working day. Delays can mean that to keep up a reasonable frequency an extra bus must be used – an expensive matter in providing and maintaining the bus and paying its drivers even if, with the persistent staff shortage, drivers can be found for it.

The fare-collection problem is not confined to London Transport – it is one of the greatest difficulties being experienced in bus undertakings all over the country and has recently been studied by a Working Group set up by the Minister for Transport Industries. Its report, issued in November 1971, recommended that a study should be initiated into the whole question of passenger handling systems, including vehicle layout and fares systems, and their effect on boarding times – a project which should be undertaken by an independent organization and carried out in full liaison with related work already in progress in the bus industry.

One-man-operation is, of course, almost the only way of increasing productivity open to the bus operator, but as far as London Transport is concerned the staff who have transferred to o.m.o. work have almost all welcomed the change. Apart from the better pay, they have enjoyed being in closer contact with the public instead of sitting in a lonely and isolated cab with no company but the constantly ringing bell. From the management point of view, o.m.o. reduces the number of staff required but enables those remaining to be better paid, helping to retain existing staff and attract others into the industry.

The importance of the effect of traffic congestion on buses is at last being understood and cities in many parts of the world are seeking ways of giving public transport priority. One of the principal means is by setting aside traffic lanes in busy roads, with or against the general flow, for the exclusive – or almost exclusive – use of buses. Paris has getting on for a hundred such lanes. The argument for them is that buses carry many people whereas peak-hour cars usually carry only the driver – or at most one passenger. The bus lane, therefore, gives priority to *people* rather than vehicles. A start has now been made on the provision of bus lanes in London and by the time this book appears there may be as many as 30 in operation.

Another potential weapon in the fight against congestion was forged when in August 1970 the Minister of Transport introduced new regulations providing for desig-

Interior of a 'DMS' bus showing the 'self-service' ticket-issuing equipment and tripod-type entry gate to saloon

nated bus stop areas to be treated as 'clearways' between 07 00 and 19 00. A large number of stops – some 700 – have been nominated by London Transport but the necessary road marking by local authorities is slow in being carried out. At the end of 1971 the only ones introduced were at Ealing where special traffic management measures were introduced to assist the congestion-hit E3 flat-fare route. London Transport would have preferred a complete ban on parking at bus stops but this half-way stage is obviously of very considerable assistance. Bus bays have been provided in many parts of London but these are primarily to assist other traffic to pass while buses are standing at stops. With the longer stops necessitated by one-man working they are more useful than ever.

London Transport has erected many roadside shelters at busy or exposed stops and has made a financial contribution in suitable cases to help local councils to erect shelters of their own. In recent years the local advertising potential of shelters has been recognized and in some parts of London advertising

The special canopy over Victoria Bus Station for all-weather protection of bus passengers

firms, with the agreement of local councils, are erecting shelters free in return for the sole advertising rights. In furtherance of the policy of improving interchange facilities, London Transport has erected large canopies over the bus stations at Victoria and Hounslow and has made arrangements to erect a similar canopy at London Bridge when development plans for the main-line station have been brought to a suitable state. Another interchange complex is being built at Finsbury Park.

Right at the end of 1970 the Chairman of London Transport, Sir Richard Way, broke a bottle of champagne over the first of the new one-man operated double-deck buses to be built for London Transport especially for operation by one man, naming it the 'Londoner'. As before, the alteration in regulations which allowed double-deckers to be single-manned had left London Transport no time in which to design and test a bus of its own if immediate and urgent advantage were to be taken of the new rule.

The 'Londoner' bus, nearly 2,000 of which should be on the roads by 1975, has seats for 44 passengers on the upper deck and 24 on the lower deck, with space for 21 standing. There is a split entrance as on some of the buses already described and the staircase is opposite the central exit so that alighting passengers are clear of it before those boarding begin to ascend. Other features include fluorescent lighting, a fresh air heating and ventilating system with automatic temperature control, and a public address system. The driver controls the power-operated entrance and exit doors and has a periscope to enable him to see whether there are still seats vacant on the upper deck.

The bus is 30ft. 10in. long, 8ft. 2½in. wide, and 14ft. 6in. high, and the body (built by Park Royal or, in some later models, by Metro-Cammell Weymann) is carried on a Leyland Daimler 'Fleetline' chassis. All the earlier buses are powered by a six-cylinder Gardner diesel engine, mounted transversely at the rear, developing 170 b.h.p. at 1,850 r.p.m., but some later models will have Leyland engines. The transmission, as on other London buses in the past 15 years, is through a fluid flywheel and a fully automatic air-operated epicyclic gearbox. Further help for the driver is given by the power-assisted steering. These 'Londoners', or 'DMS' buses, are London's buses of the immediate future. The first batch entered service on 2 January 1971 on routes 95 and 220.

In 1971, the last complete year before this book was itself completed, London Transport was able to declare that it had provided a better service than it had in the previous year. Another 600 new buses came into service and the number of miles lost through staff shortages decreased by nearly a third. The Government announced that it would increase its grants for new buses from 25 per cent. of the cost to 50 per cent. and the Greater London Council made considerable contributions to capital expenditure. There was no general fares increase in 1971 despite very considerable rises in costs of all kinds but there was a rise on 2 January 1972 and another on 10 September 1972, though not all fares were affected at each increase.

Because London Transport also operates one of the largest and most important urban

A 'DMS' type one-man-operated double-deck bus crossing Westminster Bridge in 1972

London's first minibus service is shown here at the Green, Winchmore Hill, on the first day of operation in 1972

railway systems in the world, the somewhat artificial 'hiving-off' of the bus operations adopted perforce in this book make detailed discussion of finance and fares impossible without referring to many non-bus matters.

Bus operation, with so many O.M.O. vehicles (over 1,400 at the end of 1971) now in service, has reached the point where although there is still a severe staff shortage the clearance of traffic congestion has become even more important. The new 'Londoner' (or 'DMS') buses seem to have been accepted by passengers much more willingly than the single-deckers, the last of which were received in November 1971.

Yet another problem has beset London Transport recently with the newer buses. They have proved to be much less reliable mechanically than their predecessors built especially for London service to London Transport's own designs instead of, with minor modifications, being standard public service vehicle designs. It is being proved true that London conditions really *are* different from those elsewhere in the country with miles of operations passing through built-up local centre after local centre, each equivalent to the single town centre of many a provincial city. Following industrial troubles in the manufacturing industries, a grave shortage of spare parts developed which has still not been completely overcome and there have been waits of nine months or a year for some spares. In an exercise reminiscent of the similar difficulties just after the last war, London Transport has had to resort to cannibalization, special reconditioning of parts in its own workshops, and even manufacture of parts to keep the single-deck fleet going. A world shortage of the long-fibre type of asbestos used for brake linings had such an effect that London Transport's own research and development staff had to set to work to find an alternative. After over 400 tests on service buses, they found three suitable variants which would maintain the essential high standard of braking required.

The 'split-entrance' type of working has been one of the most successful of the fare collection systems, as has already been mentioned, but the equipment installed for the 'self-service' channel proved unreliable and many became so inefficient in time that the channel they served had to be closed off on some routes and all passengers had to pay the driver, with a consequent slowing down of boarding and of the time taken to cover the route as a whole. It must, of course, be realized that London Transport and its bus passengers were all operating in a relatively untried field with equipment working at an intensity probably unmatched elsewhere. However, new equipment with a much improved performance has been developed in co-operation with London Transport engineers and this new machine is being fitted to all the 'DMS' vehicles. It has resulted in greater use as passengers have realized its reliability and their confidence has been restored. Research into these problems is still being pressed on by London Transport as well as other operators. Meanwhile it was announced in November 1972 that the difficulties of one-man bus operation in Central London were such as to render the service unacceptable to the public. For the time being, therefore, it is proposed that two-man buses, with a conductor, will continue to operate on the busiest routes working through the central area.

Another experiment was carried out on three Ealing flat-fare routes to gauge the effect on boarding times. On their first journey passengers could buy a strip of eight tickets for 30p. Together with the initial journey, for which no ticket was taken, passengers could make nine journeys for 30p, a reduction of 6p or more than 16% on the usual fares. On the second and subsequent journeys passengers tore off one of the eight sections of 'multi-ride' ticket and inserted it in the fare-box on the bus instead of paying cash. Operational research studies towards the end of 1971 showed that, while a significant proportion of passengers had bought the multi-ride tickets, there had been no worthwhile improvement in the speed of boarding or amount of change-giving by the driver. Nevertheless, a further step has been taken in arranging that four-ride tickets, costing 14p – a reduction of 12½ per cent. – should be sold at local shops. This experiment began on 20 November 1972.

Towards the end of 1971 a special experimental bus unit was set up to deal with developments in radio control and vehicle location systems, and to consider possible experiments with new ways of running buses. Such experiments might, for example, involve buses of various sizes (including minibuses), variations in routeing, and 'dial-a-bus'.

London Transport has long been urged to try experimental minibus routes but has been deterred from doing so because, among other things, a small bus needs a driver in just the same way as a large one and the driver could be more productively employed on a larger vehicle. No cost savings would be made if another suggestion often put forward – of using large vehicles in the peaks, and small ones in the off-peak – were followed since this would mean buying and maintaining more vehicles. The running cost difference between small and large o.m.o. buses is not sufficient to counterbalance the very large capital expenditure which would be needed. Nevertheless, with the financial backing of the Greater London Council, four minibus services, using 16-seat buses with Strachan bodies on Ford chassis, are being tried. The first (W9) began operations between Enfield and Southgate on 9 September 1972 and the others – a cross-Camden link and services in the Dulwich and Elmstead Woods areas – followed shortly afterwards. The routes were carefully chosen to test the demand for minibus travel in different types of area where there was insufficient demand for a normal bus service. All the routes have a 10p flat fare paid into fare collection boxes next to the driver.

Mileage lost through traffic congestion – still one of London Transport's most serious problems – gives only a general indication

and does not reveal the disruption of schedules in the London area occurring every day and the effect on the reliability of the services. The volume of private cars and other traffic on roads has brought things very near saturation point so that a vehicle breakdown or collision, or a lorry shedding its load can rapidly lead to major hold-ups. Faulty traffic lights, burst water mains, and fires with consequent road closures and delays, can dislocate bus services either temporarily or for quite long periods. Gaps in service and bunching of buses follow and have the effect of destroying the public's confidence in the services. The following report – not originally intended for publication or anything but internal use – tells the story of one such day:

To

CHIEF OPERATING MANAGER (Buses)

From

TRAFFIC SUPERINTENDENT (Buses)

Date 4 April 1972

'OPERATION ON MAUNDY THURSDAY, MARCH 30, 1972.

'An increase in general vehicular traffic on this day brought many thoroughfares to a virtual standstill from the latter part of the morning throughout the day until about 1900 hours.

'The delays were so serious that, in order to avoid mechanical failures due to overheating, drivers were asked to switch off their engines if it seemed that traffic was unlikely to move within a reasonable period of time. It was reported that one bus at least on service 15 was stationary with engine switched off in the Edgware Road for a full hour. On this particular service buses running between Aldgate and Ladbroke Grove were taking an average of nearly five hours to make the round trip instead of the two hours allowed, the longest time taken being six hours. In consequence, the service was running at only a third of the scheduled frequency.

'There were many prolonged gaps on the services in Central London and, as a guide to the effects, a selection of examples has been tabulated and is appended. In the case of the trunk cross-London services, it was found possible in some cases to use a small number of buses to provide a restricted service at the suburban ends. Since many buses were "locked up" in the traffic, our through passengers experienced some considerable gaps. Where buses were not getting through at all from Central London our officials were powerless.

'As can be seen from the notes on the appendix, some services were running two to three hours late on average and this meant that staff were not able to carry out their second spell of duty, thus exacerbating an already difficult position.

'The suburban areas also suffered badly on this day. . . .'

What of the future?

Most of the guide-lines for the immediate future have now been laid down. Given the staff and the reasonably rapid implementation of the ideas and plans already in being, the fall in traffic, already considerably slowed down, should be arrested. As surveys have shown, the thing passengers value above all in bus services is reliability. The measures laid down should eventually restore this, especially if even more priority can be given to buses by, say, fitting them with a device to bias traffic lights in their favour. The most important way in which passengers can help is by having the right money ready, in the right coins, as they board their bus.

The bus may never again be the bulk carrier it was just after the war when motor cars were comparatively rare, and for longer journeys the Underground, with its own reserved track, will always be faster, but the whole reason for the being of the bus is its capacity for picking up passengers at the street corner for a short trip to the shops, the station, the hospital, the friend a mile or so away. For many years Londoners have been primarily short-distance bus riders. For these journeys the bus is, and will long remain, supreme.

Bibliography

BARKER, L. C. AND ROBBINS, MICHAEL	*London Transport, A History of (Vols. 1 & 2)*	*1963/73*
BRUCE, J. GRAEME AND CURTIS, C. H.	*London Motor Bus, The*	*1973*
GILLHAM, JOHN C.	*London's Double Deck Buses*	*1950*
GRAVES, CHARLES	*London Transport Carried On*	*1947*
KENNEDY, BASIL C. AND MARSHALL, P. J.	*London Bus 1933-1957, The*	*1957*
KIDNER, R. W.	*London Motor Bus 1896-1949, The*	*1950*
LEE, CHARLES E.	*Horse Bus as a Vehicle, The*	*1962*
LEE, CHARLES E.	*Early Motor Bus, The*	*1962*
MOORE, H. C.	*Omnibuses and Cabs*	*1902*
MORRIS, O. J.	*Fares Please*	*1953*
PRICE, J. H.	*London Buses in Wartime*	*1965*
PRICE, J. H.	*London General*	*1956*
ROBBINS, G. J. AND ATKINSON, J. B.	*London 'B' Type Motor Omnibus, The*	*1971*
SOMMERFIELD, VERNON	*London's Buses*	*1933*
STRONG, L. A. G.	*Rolling Road, The*	*1956*
WAGSTAFF, J. S.	*London RT Bus, The*	*1972*

INDEX

[141]